"In this helpful commentary, significance of the Chronicles' fictive characters and happenings, showing how they are rich with spiritual values."

— Dr. Vernon C. Grounds
chancellor, Denver Seminary

"Robert Velarde has provided readers with an incredibly thorough, insightful, and detailed examination of the ethical principles and theological concepts underlying the imaginative tales of the Chronicles of Narnia. *The Heart of Narnia* is as accessible as it is erudite and accurate. Every fan of Lewis will want to own a copy."

— Jim Ware
author of *God of the Fairy Tale*

"Robert Velarde's *The Heart of Narnia* is an outstanding study of the philosophical, ethical, and theological principles that underlie C. S. Lewis's Chronicles of Narnia, enabling readers to connect their encounter with Aslan in the world of Narnia with the Christ we encounter in our own world. A must-read for Lewis fans of all theological persuasions."

— Victor Reppert, PhD
author of *C. S. Lewis's Dangerous Idea*

The HEART of NARNIA

WISDOM, VIRTUE, *and* LIFE LESSONS
from the CLASSIC CHRONICLES

ROBERT VELARDE

NAVPRESS®

The Navigators is an international Christian organization. Our mission is to advance the gospel of Jesus and His kingdom into the nations through spiritual generations of laborers living and discipling among the lost. We see a vital movement of the gospel, fueled by prevailing prayer, flowing freely through relational networks and out into the nations where workers for the kingdom are next door to everywhere.

NavPress is the publishing ministry of The Navigators. The mission of NavPress is to reach, disciple, and equip people to know Christ and make Him known by publishing life-related materials that are biblically rooted and culturally relevant. Our vision is to stimulate spiritual transformation through every product we publish.

ISBN-13: 978-1-60006-238-4
ISBN-10: 1-60006-238-5

Cover design by The DesignWorks Group
Creative Team: Don Simpson, Arvid Wallen, Eric Stanford, Cara Iverson, Pat Reinheimer

CIP DATA APPLIED FOR

Printed in the United States of America

1 2 3 4 5 6 7 8 / 12 11 10 09 08

For Anthony, Vincent, and Dante

May you enter Narnia as you are and return better than you were.

Contents

ACKNOWLEDGMENTS

I would like to thank Vernon Grounds for allowing me to serve as his assistant for a Denver Seminary course on the philosophy of C. S. Lewis — the course that sparked the idea for this book. I am grateful as well to Douglas Groothuis, Gordon Lewis, Rich Poll, Lela Satterfield, and Peter Schakel for words of encouragement and advice at various stages of the project. Thanks also go to Don Simpson and Eric Stanford for their editorial support. Special appreciation belongs to Will Vaus, who proofread several chapters and offered his lucid insights. My wife, Candace, not only provided encouraging words but also proofread the manuscript and put up with the book's all-encompassing impact on my life. Her love and intellect are my constant companions, and for that I am abundantly thankful. Finally, I would like to thank my children, to whom this book is dedicated, for tolerating Dad's need for space and time. I'm glad we were able to travel to Narnia together again while I took breaks from my writing.

Although I had a great deal of support on this project, any deficiencies in the text are mine alone.

Introduction

In a quiet, snowy wood at night, a small and curious-looking creature, appearing like a man from the waist up but with legs like a goat, approaches a solitary lamppost, its light shining incongruously among the trees. He is so startled by the presence of a creature he has only read about in books (it just might be a human child) that he drops several packages he is carrying, though he retains his grip on an umbrella. Tumnus is a faun in the fairy-tale land of Narnia and is the first creature that eight-year-old Lucy Pevensie encounters after she has entered Narnia through a magical wardrobe in *The Lion, the Witch and the Wardrobe.*[1] After a brief discussion with Lucy at the lamppost, Tumnus invites her to his home for tea. While she is there, she scans some of the books on a shelf and notes their peculiar titles, such as *Is Man a Myth?* To Tumnus, humans are legendary or mythological; conversely, humans consider fauns to be mythical creatures. Yet here they both are, living comfortably together in a world of fantasy.

There is no disputing the recent surge in popularity of fantasy literature. J. K. Rowling's Harry Potter books and films, motion pictures based on the Lord of the Rings trilogy by J. R. R. Tolkien, and films bringing to life *The Chronicles of Narnia,* by C. S. Lewis, are but a few factors contributing to this resurgence of interest. Without a doubt there is something broadly attractive in fantasy stories — something that appealed to Lewis's longing for fulfillment. As a fan of fantasy literature, and especially as one who has loved the Chronicles of Narnia ever since I discovered them as a college sophomore, I, too, am pleased to observe this renewed popularity of fantasy.

But despite the trend in the sales of movie tickets and books, I have noticed there is a popular misconception concerning works such as the Chronicles. Many have the idea that the books are only for children and that when one grows up, such "children's books" are no longer of value. Those with this mindset believe that as people grow to adulthood, they should move on to more important matters than the interests of childhood. Among other things, this means leaving imaginative "children's literature" behind.

The more literarily astute, such as Lewis, recognize that a good book remains a good book regardless of its classification. With the possible exception of reference works, Lewis believed, the contemporary distinctions between adult and children's books, particularly the association of fantasy with children, is artificial. To think it proper only for children to read these kinds of books is a recent and false distinction, according to Lewis. He pointed out that most of the great fairy tales were not addressed to children specifically but to readers of all ages.[2] Walter Hooper observed that Lewis "wrote fairy tales simply because he liked them himself and because he found them the best art form for what he had to say."[3] Consequently, while most children thoroughly enjoy the Chronicles of Narnia, there is much in them to be savored and pondered by adults.

If you have read any of the seven books of the Chronicles, you already have some idea of the charm of the stories. At first glance, they appear to be only for children, but hidden within the pages (sometimes not so hidden) are treasures of deep philosophical, theological, and especially moral value. For example, *The Silver Chair* presents several intriguing similarities to Plato's famous allegory of the cave, and Aslan's death at the Stone Table in *The Lion, the Witch and the Wardrobe* reflects the sacrificial death of Christ on the cross. Certainly there is a danger of reading too much into the stories, or "using" them instead of "receiving" them, as Lewis would say;[4] nevertheless, the books are rich in meaning on several levels. The Chronicles are marvelous artistic achievements that appeal not only to the *heart* via imagination and wonder but also to the *head* via reason and intellectual astuteness.

The Heart of Narnia will explore the ethics of this popular series—what it tells us about right and wrong ways of behaving. If you have not read the Chronicles of Narnia, I encourage you to do so, but even if you haven't, you will still benefit from this book (though, in that case, it will help to first review the plot summaries of the Chronicles in the appendix). *The Heart of Narnia* will provide you with a fascinating look at the Golden Rules of Narnia and at key points made about virtue and vice throughout the series. The Narnia books were not intended as ethical instruction manuals per se, but they *are* filled with lessons for both casual and careful readers. They teach us how our everyday decisions contribute to the development of our moral character, whether for good or ill. Furthermore, they show that individuals having the courage to act on their moral beliefs can have an impact on social events and even the course of history.

Morality is serious business. Good and evil are at war in this world, and the choices we make really do matter. Sometimes shocking to the first-time reader of the series, the Chronicles show us numerous contests and battles: Aslan against the White Witch, Rilian against the queen of Underland, the Calormenes against the forces of Archenland, and many more. The children themselves often participate in these battles, having to struggle and suffer and sometimes enduring wounds. But they — and we, the readers — learn in the process that evil must be opposed with courage and fortitude.

Many fairy tales depict a world of violence and evil. As Jim Ware wrote,

> When we travel in the company of fairy-tale heroes or heroines, we soon find that the world is far more dangerous and sinister than we had suspected. . . . This vision of the world as a kind of Venus's-flytrap — bright, beautiful, and malevolent — is fundamental to fairy stories. . . . Evil is an ever-present threat in the land of Faerie. In fact, the unspeakable glory and light of that land owe their power largely to the contrasting darkness and ugliness of its less attractive corners.[5]

This element of fairy tales has caused some concern among parents. Why must fairy tales depict violence, evil, and the dark side of life? By doing so, Ware points out, fairy tales are able to effectively communicate the power of light as well as the power of darkness.[6] In the Christian view, it is true that the world is fractured, but it is also true that light still shines in the darkness (see John 1:5).

In responding to concerns over serious elements in fairy tales, especially the charge that such stories will frighten children, C. S. Lewis argued that because children will at some point encounter such evils in the real world, there is nothing wrong with allowing them to be exposed to evil via fairy tales, so long as good prevails in the end.[7] Lewis was not advocating gratuitous and graphic violence, of course, but he was concerned with giving children a view of the reality of evil in the world. It is significant that in Lewis's stories evil is overcome, for a fairy tale in which evil consistently overcomes good offers little hope. Children and adults can come away from his stories with a better understanding of positive moral behavior. For Lewis, the genre of Narnia (that is, fairy tales) called for the exploration of themes of good and evil.

In a world where dictators store nuclear weapons in their arsenals, where fanatics plot how to bring terror to our doorsteps, where the end of the world wars and the Cold War has brought no end to fighting, it is easy to see that the battle between good and evil exists and must be engaged. On a more personal level, we can see how individual choices to do what is wrong can lead to destruction: CEO hubris bringing down corporations, selfishness resulting in the devastation of the family, and sexual promiscuity spreading fatal diseases are only a few examples. It may be, in fact, that we live in a world more ready than ever for the kind of moral guidance offered by the deceptively simple tales of Narnia.

Indeed, there have been times when people were inclined to believe that standards of morality are unimportant and that ethical choices should be left to personal taste. But more and more, we are realizing that good and evil are real and that it makes a difference which side we choose to line up on. The everyday choices we make are turning us into people who are helping the good cause to win or who are standing in the way of the good. In this light, the Chronicles are not only great fun to read but also eminently useful in showing us how we ought to live—for our own well-being and that of all of society.

Let us, then, go through the wardrobe ourselves, enter Narnia, and see what we can learn there about right living that we can use when we get back to *our* world.

CHAPTER 1

GOOD *and* EVIL *in* NARNIA

The Last Battle — the final volume of the Chronicles of Narnia — is dark and sad, especially for those who love Narnia and are reading the book for the first time. Beyond the hint in the title, the opening words of the book, "In the last days of Narnia," are disconcerting.[1] Not much later, Tirian is referred to as the last king of Narnia. The reader senses that something dreadful is going to happen. But what? The warlike Calormenes, who have formed an alliance with a traitorous ape named Shift, have secretly been entering Narnia and are bent on conquest. Surely the great lion Aslan will send help, won't he? And so he does send aid by way of Eustace Scrubb and Jill Pole. But it is not enough. The Calormenes are victorious, and Narnia comes to an end. The story, however, does not end. Evil exists, but as in Christianity, good will ultimately prevail.

It is not only in the final volume but also all the way through the Chronicles of Narnia that we see themes of good and evil displayed. Characters are presented with challenges and choices and must make a decision about how to act. What they decide to do has repercussions in their own lives and the lives of those with whom they are connected. All this sounds a lot like our own life stories, doesn't it? Indeed, our daily ethical challenges, both great and small, are reflected in many ways in the pages of the Chronicles. Without forgetting that we are reading a made-up narrative, and certainly without losing a sense of the fun of it all, we can learn valuable lessons in morality from these seven classic tales.

In the chapters that follow, we will look at what are, for the most part, pairs of ethical opposites—virtues and vices—as reflected in the Chronicles of Narnia. These will help us wrangle with specific ethical issues that each of us must face in life. Before that, though, it will be helpful to gain an overall view of C. S. Lewis's ethical beliefs, especially as they are reflected in the Chronicles. The first thing to note is that Lewis was by no means infected by the modern (or, more accurately, postmodern) hesitancy in calling wrong, wrong.

MORAL ABSOLUTES

Most people would condemn such things as rape, child abuse, and terrorism. But why? (Or, more disturbingly, why not?) On what basis do we determine right and wrong? Do cultural conventions set the standards? Or could it be that a God exists and is the source of such standards for all people at all times? Ethics is the branch of philosophy concerned with right and wrong and, consequently, with how one should or should not live.

In *Mere Christianity*, Lewis explained that as an atheist, he argued against God on the basis of evil and suffering in the world. He asked how he had gotten the idea of what is just and unjust, reasoning that in order to consider something as wrong, one must have a concept of right. But where does this standard come from?[2] Following his conversion to Christianity, Lewis often made the case for objective moral truth. He was aware of fine ethical distinctions and moral ambiguities, but, more basically, he wanted to affirm the difference between good and evil. Paul Ford correctly observed in reference to morality in Narnia, "Lewis believed there was a clear distinction between right and wrong; between morality and immorality; and between good acts and bad acts."[3]

Lewis wrote before postmodernism had gained the popularity it did in the late twentieth century. His position on moral absolutes reflected the earlier, "modern" view that truth (meaning truth that is valid for all times and in all places) really exists and can really be known. Later thinkers in the postmodern vein were more likely to view truth and morality as relative to culture and to individual situations or tastes. Alan Jacobs elaborated, "Lewis wrote in a time when, among the educated British public if not among their professional philosophers, there was considerably more agreement than there is now about, for instance, what constitutes a valid and rational argument for a given case. . . . His apologetic works presuppose, and rarely make any argument for, the criteria for rationality themselves. Today those criteria simply cannot be assumed."[4]

These days, Lewis's argument for objective moral law would have to be bolstered for those influenced by relativistic ethics. But it may be that the climate of our day is warming again to ideas of definite right and wrong. Lewis's words still resonate with those who sense the danger of an ethic in which any type of behavior might be acceptable under the right circumstances. As old-fashioned as the ideas of virtue and vice in the Chronicles of Narnia might at first appear to be, they speak to an eternal need to know how to act when we are faced with a choice. Few books can inspire us so well with the courage to do what is right as can these simple tales. Maybe their underlying philosophy is not weak or outmoded after all.

Of course, Lewis did not develop his ethical ideas without the influence of past thinkers. While a thorough analysis of the philosophical influences on C. S. Lewis is beyond the scope of this chapter, it will be beneficial to gain at least a basic understanding of these influences.[5]

Great Thinkers Who Influenced Lewis

Lewis was clearly moved by the likes of English journalist and writer G. K. Chesterton (1874–1936) and Scottish novelist George MacDonald (1824–1905).[6] Some elements of the philosophy of Immanuel Kant (1724–1804) are also reflected in Lewis's ethical concepts. As Armand Nicholi has observed, "Lewis agrees with German philosopher Immanuel Kant, who pointed to the 'moral law within' as a powerful witness to the greatness of God."[7] But the greater philosophical influences on Lewis were classical philosophers. Gilbert Meilaender rightly explained, "Lewis' views are best characterized not by reference to contemporary thinkers but . . . by reference to Augustine, Plato, and Aristotle."[8] So great were the influences of Plato and Aristotle on Lewis that he once wrote that losing the influence of these two philosophers would be like the amputation of a limb.[9]

Plato believed in the unchanging world of Ideas or Forms. Because ethical standards are derived from this unchanging standard, Plato concluded that ethical standards are also unchanging. Similarly, Lewis believed there are transcendent, universal, and unchanging standards rooted in natural law. Moreover, like Plato, Lewis believed that the current world is not all there is — that a better, more real world awaits us. As Lewis has a character say in *Till We Have Faces,* "Nothing is yet in its true form."[10] Lewis also affirmed his affinity for Plato in *The Last Battle.* When Narnia is destroyed, it is revealed that Aslan's country contains the real Narnia — bigger and more beautiful than the "copy" or "shadow" that was destroyed. The character Digory Kirke makes the connection obvious when he says of the discovery that he has entered the *real* Narnia that it is all explained in Plato.[11]

Lewis also owed much to Plato's pupil Aristotle. Aristotle believed that in the pursuit of ultimate good or happiness, ethical standards require a balance between extremes — a golden mean — of vice and virtue. According to Aristotle, developing moral character is more important than following strict rules of conduct. What matters is living a virtuous life based on reason. Consequently, virtuous moral choices are desirable and, if habitually made, will shape our character for the better. Lewis, too, was more concerned with the virtuous life and the importance of our daily choices in given situations than he was with adherence to specific ethical commands.

Despite these influences by Aristotle and Plato, Meilaender considered Lewis's overarching social and ethical views "as, quite simply, Augustinian," referring to the African theologian

Augustine.[12] In *The Four Loves,* Lewis called Augustine a great thinker to whom he owed a tremendous debt.[13] Lewis, like Augustine, viewed evil as a privation. Good exists, but when the good is missing, the result is evil. Lewis often referred to evil as parasitical on good or as a perversion of it, such as in a 1933 letter in which he referred to evil as "good *spoiled.*"[14] Ethically, Augustine believed in transcendent and unchanging standards that have their source in a personal, active God who has revealed Himself not only in general revelation (evidence of God in nature or human conscience) but also in special revelation (such as in the Bible and the Incarnation). Lewis would agree with these points as well as with Augustine's position that happiness can be found only in God. Also, like Augustine, Lewis's ethics were built upon a foundation of love. Lewis agreed that true longing and, hence, happiness can be found only in God. In commenting on the Golden Rule ("Do to others what you would have them do to you," Matthew 7:12), Lewis acknowledged that repeating this phrase is meaningless unless one is able to love his or her neighbor — a task that cannot be carried out unless one first loves God.[15] This is an Augustinian view requiring obedience as well as love.

In at least one area of his ethics, Lewis appears to have owed more to Scripture than to any philosopher or theologian. That area is what is known as "the problem of evil." Given that the biblical God is all-loving as well as all-powerful, why does evil exist?

THE PROBLEM OF EVIL

The Old Testament prophet Isaiah wrote,

> Woe to those who call evil good
> and good evil. (Isaiah 5:20)

Biblically, it is clear that good and evil exist, as do moral distinctions between them. The story of the Bible is the story of a struggle between good and evil, with good ultimately prevailing over evil as our world draws to a close. In an Augustinian sense, our world is not the best possible world, but it is the best way to the best possible world. Hence, evil exists, but it will finally be vanquished. While some have accused Christianity of promoting a sort of dualism between God and Satan, Christian theism does not truly promote such a dualism, because Satan is a created being and his power does not match that of God, who is all-powerful, all-knowing, and ever-present. But in that case, why does evil exist?

The Greek philosopher Epicurus phrased the problem of evil as follows:

> God either wishes to take away evils, and is unable; or he is able and unwilling; or he is neither willing nor able, or he is both willing and able. If he is willing and is unable, he is feeble, which is not in accordance with the character of God; if he is able and unwilling, he is envious, which is equally at variance with God; if he is neither willing nor able he is both envious and feeble and therefore not God; if he is both willing and able, which alone is suitable to God, from what source then are evils? or why does he not remove them?[16]

The basic problem is how to explain the presence of evil and suffering in light of the existence of an all-powerful and loving God.

Intellectually, Lewis addressed this topic in *The Problem of Pain*.[17] Emotionally, he grappled with the matter in *A Grief Observed*.[18] His beliefs were nicely nuanced, and he certainly did not minimize the complexity of the problem. He admitted that Christianity does not necessarily have a neat or complete explanation for the problem of evil, but he said that Christianity's explanation is far better than others. He affirmed the biblical picture that, in the grand view, God is in the process of redeeming the good and establishing justice for all time. Through Christ's suffering, a way has been made to rescue the repentant and punish the incorrigibly wicked.

This view of God's sympathy for and activity on behalf of the suffering is implicitly addressed in the Chronicles. One example is Digory's mother, Mabel, and her serious illness—something that grieves Aslan. The death of Caspian in *The Silver Chair* is another example. Caspian dies, but he arrives in Aslan's country (heaven) submerged in water and is revived by the blood of the lion—a distinctly Christian image no doubt inspired by the concept of being cleansed by the blood of Christ (see, for example, Hebrews 9:13-15). Aslan weeps for Mabel and Caspian, thus expressing God's sympathy for the human predicament. (Recall that Jesus wept for Lazarus and, by extension, for the human condition, as told in John 11:1-44.)

History is a stage on which God is working out His final solution to the problem of evil. In the Chronicles of Narnia, Christ is represented by Aslan, while His opponent, Satan, is represented most nearly by the White Witch, Jadis.

THE LION AND THE WITCH

In Aslan and the White Witch, we see the personification of the struggle between right and wrong, good and evil. This is not an interplay of two abstract concepts but the interaction of two individual characters in Narnian history. Reflected in their relationship is the drama that God is writing in terrestrial history as He prepares for the final defeat of evil.

In each of the Chronicles, Aslan the lion is the centerpiece of all that is good, holy, and just. Other characters may embody these traits, but not nearly to the same extent and not consistently. Aslan stands for virtue, condemns vice, and is clearly a Christ figure, though not in a strictly allegorical sense. In *The Lion, the Witch and the Wardrobe,* he willingly sacrifices his life to save the human child Edmund from death. In *Prince Caspian,* Aslan participates in the overthrow of the evil usurping King Miraz, while in *The Voyage of the "Dawn Treader,"* he is present in many instances of good, for example, in a powerful encounter with Eustace and as the source of Reepicheep's longing. In a scene in *The Silver Chair* reminiscent of Jesus' discussion with the Samaritan woman at the well described in John 4, Aslan speaks with Jill Pole on issues related to salvation and once again seeks, through those who serve him, to overcome evil with good, restoring Prince Rilian and, in the process, destroying the evil witch of the Underworld. In *The Horse and His Boy*, the four principal characters — Shasta, Bree, Aravis, and Hwin — each learn ethical lessons from Aslan regarding humility and pride. When Shasta is alone with Aslan, the great lion explains the role he has played in the boy's life, always watching over him.

The White Witch (Jadis in *The Magician's Nephew*) is not an opposite of Aslan in a dualistic sense. She is a created being from another world who enters Narnia at the time of its creation. There are some parallels to the Christian account of Satan, such as the witch tempting Digory in the garden, but they should not be pressed to the point of actually equating the witch with Satan, as there are simply too many differences. That the witch is evil is clear. Aslan himself refers to her as evil in *The Magician's Nephew,*[19] and she exhibits a number of vices indicating her evil nature: unfairness, dishonesty, pride, cruelty, a warlike nature, and impenitence.

Those characters in the Chronicles who are allied with Aslan act more like him, while those who are the witch's helpers reflect her own evil propensities. So it is for us. There are good behaviors (virtues) and bad behaviors (vices). We can choose whom we follow and how we will act.

Vices and Virtues in Narnia

Lewis believed that everyday ethical decisions move one closer in character to good or evil. As a result, even the small ethical decisions made daily are, in the long run, incredibly important. These decisions for good or evil accrue in our character like a savings account earning compound interest, said Lewis, indicating that a series of decisions for the good, however small, may accumulate over time and result in a good ethical decision in the future.[20] Or, conversely, a series of small evil decisions will build up, tarnishing one's character and allowing entry for further (and likely increased) evil. Lewis elaborated on this matter in

Mere Christianity, in which he wrote, "Every time you make a choice you are turning the central part of you . . . into something a little different from what it was before." Over the course of a lifetime, we are turning this central part of ourselves into either a "heavenly creature" or a "hellish creature."[21]

In that same work, Lewis gave an illustration involving tennis. He noted that even a person who does not play tennis well may make a lucky shot now and then, but a good player has the training and experience that allows him or her to make numerous good shots and become someone whose tennis skill can be relied upon. Similarly, a person who regularly practices virtuous behavior will attain a godly quality of character.[22] This quality and not specific actions, argued Lewis, is virtue.

In *The Magician's Nephew,* because of the actions of a boy named Digory Kirke, evil has entered the new world of Narnia in the form of Jadis (the White Witch). Aslan the lion asks Digory if he is prepared to undo the wrong he has caused.[23] Digory tells Aslan that he is ready to do what he can. Then his thoughts turn to his mother, who lies dying a world away. With eyes full of tears, the twelve-year-old Digory asks Aslan to help his mother. Tears fill Aslan's eyes, too, for he is acquainted with grief. But the lion informs Digory that Narnia must be protected from evil, at least for a time, and that Digory must retrieve an apple from a tree in a distant garden so that a tree may be planted on earth for the protection of Narnia.

Riding upon the flying horse, Fledge, Digory and his friend Polly begin an adventure that leads them to a beautiful valley. At the top of a hill, they come to a wall with golden gates. They realize that this is a private, perhaps even sacred, place. A message written on the gates warns that entrance to the garden is permitted only by the gates and that the fruit within must be taken only to help others.[24]

Digory approaches the gates, which open as he places a hand on them, and enters the garden alone. He plucks a silver apple from a tree and is tempted by the fruit's appearance and smell. Why not take another one? Maybe the words on the gate were meant more as advice and not as rules, he thinks. As he glances around, he sees a strange bird in a tree watching him lazily with one eye barely open. For some reason, that sight helps him decide to obey Aslan, despite his longing for the silver apple.

As he begins to leave the garden, he sees the witch. Her mouth is stained with the juice of a silver apple, and she tosses away the core. Her skin has turned white. Digory runs away, but the witch is after him. He stops and threatens to return to his world then and there by the use of magic. Jadis tries to convince him to eat an apple because it has the power of youth as well as of life. If he does, he can rule the world as king, with her as his queen. This offer fails to induce Digory to eat the apple.

Next, Jadis tries another tack in her temptation of the boy. She tries to convince Digory to take an apple back to his mother so that she might be healed. Digory gasps and puts a hand to his head, for he loves his mother dearly and so much wants her to be healed. He struggles with the choice, feeling the force of the terrible decision before him.[25] In the end, though, despite his desire to help his mother, Digory makes the right choice. He has made a promise to Aslan and he will not break it, no matter what.

In a way, each of us stands in a garden with forbidden fruit before us, just like Digory and just like Adam and Eve. These are the crisis points where our character is formed. The silver apple for us might be a sexual misadventure outside of marriage, an offer of illegal drugs at a party, the chance to destroy an enemy's character with a lie, or any of innumerable other options. Regardless of the nature of our temptations, if we make good choices, we become more ethical people. If we make the wrong choices, our character becomes worse and worse.

While not meant as tutorials in vice and virtue, the Chronicles of Narnia are filled with examples of both. In the chapters that follow, we will look at seven sets of characteristics as reflected in the Chronicles:

- courage and cowardice
- fairness and unfairness
- honesty and dishonesty
- mercy and cruelty
- peace and war
- humility and pride
- repentance and unrepentance

Although these are seemingly opposing traits, they are not always clearly a matter of virtue in opposition to vice. For example, Lewis would argue that engaging in warfare is not always wrong. Still, in most cases, the traits discussed in the following chapters are quite dissimilar. Hence, honesty not only is distinct from dishonesty but also is virtuous, while dishonesty is not.

What these chapters all have in common is the theme of good versus evil. In part, this is because of the nature of fantasy literature. And, in part, this is because of the nature of real life here on earth. Just as there eventually came a showdown between the Narnians and the Calormenes, and just as Digory was presented with temptation by the witch, so all of us are engaged in the contest between right and wrong. We see it in small, personal decisions as well as in the great events of world history. May we learn from Peter and Reepicheep, Shasta and Jill, Digory and Polly, and other Narnian characters, especially Aslan, how to build a character for good.

Reflection and Response Questions

1. Think of a loved one you have lost. If, like Digory, you had been offered a means to save that person's life but at the cost of defying a command of God, would you have taken the opportunity? If not, what would have kept you from disobeying God?

2. Most of us have at least one area of morality where we repeatedly let God down. It might be lust, anger, or some other sin. What is this habitual failing for you? Why do you think you tend to choose vice over virtue in this area of morality? Pray that God will use your reading of this book to place you more firmly on the side of good and not of evil.

Chapter 2

Courage *and* Cowardice

For much of *The Voyage of the "Dawn Treader,"* Eustace Scrubb is an obnoxious nuisance, prone to complaining and sulking. But something happens to Eustace on Dragon Island, and although he has relapses of his bad character, on the whole he is on his way to becoming a better person. This becomes clear one day when a sea serpent approaches the ship. Bowmen fire arrow after arrow at the ocean beast, but none penetrates its tough skin. Quickly, the giant creature begins coiling itself around the ship, intending to crush it. At this point, Eustace undertakes the first act of bravery in his life: He begins hacking at the serpent with a sword. Although his attack fails, everyone else on board, when free from the serpent, praises Eustace's valor.[1]

In Narnia, courage is a desirable virtue, while cowardice is dishonorable and shameful. A number of characters in the Chronicles exhibit either courage or cowardice. Reepicheep the talking mouse, ever ready to defend his honor and prove his bravery, is perhaps the most valiant character in the series, with Puddleglum the marsh-wiggle being another. Many human characters also exhibit courage. Among them are the four Pevensies, Caspian, and Shasta. Cowardice, too, is found in the series. Uncle Andrew reveals his cowardice in *The Magician's Nephew*, while the sailor Pittencream displays that quality in *The Voyage of the "Dawn Treader."* The curious creatures known as Duffers are cowardly to the point of recruiting a young girl to face what they believe is great danger. Clearly, C. S. Lewis considered courage to be one of the most important virtues to possess.

Courage is a desirable virtue in Narnia as well as the real world. This is particularly true when it comes to Christianity, which has a long history of valuing courage. Not only was courage numbered among the seven traditional Christian virtues, it was also one of the four cardinal virtues of the ancient Greeks.[2] And just as in the Chronicles of Narnia, courage is required in many situations of life, both in peacetime and in wartime, so the same is true for us. A normal day in an ordinary life may present one with numerous opportunities to exhibit courage or cowardice. Telling the truth when it might have a high cost, trying something that is new and risky, overcoming a longtime fear—these are only a few of the situations in which we can take a tip from the likes of Reepicheep and Eustace Scrubb and be bold. But to start with, do we really know what we mean when we talk about courage and cowardice?

FEAR: THE FIRST BATTLE

The Chronicles of Narnia are better than a dictionary at suggesting the nuances of courage and cowardice. These were subjects that Lewis had pondered deeply and wrote about eloquently, not only in the Chronicles but also in many of his other works. In this way, he helps us even today to understand more fully these opposing qualities. And if there is a single defining aspect of courage and cowardice, it lies in their different reactions to fear.

Courage is the ability to face danger fearlessly. A courageous person might feel an element of fear, but courage overcomes this fear or at least takes precedence over it. In *Mere Christianity,* Lewis included a brief mention of courage, noting that it not only faces danger but also endures pain. Moreover, he notes that other virtues will at some point require courage.[3] In *The Screwtape Letters,* Lewis offered further insights into courage, pointing out, among other things, that courage can potentially lead to pride.[4]

Cowardice lacks the qualities of courage: bravery, boldness, and valor. Giving in to fear is a key component of cowardice, as is the self-centeredness driven by such fear. This fear can be of physical pain, of psychological pain (emotional suffering), or of both. Cowardly characters in the Narnia stories, just like people in real life, are afraid of what might happen to them instead of being focused on what might happen to others.

In *The Screwtape Letters,* Lewis observed that only cowardice among all the vices is painful as well as horrible. Other vices can be put in a positive light, but cowardice is often viewed as contemptible—a reaction that increases during times of strife, such as during war. At such times, cowardice may actually work in God's favor as people acknowledge the reality of good and evil and, hence, the reality of moral issues and the state of their own character. As Screwtape puts it, challenging times have the potential to awaken thousands from their moral stupor. Screwtape also stresses that the *act* of cowardice is what devils should cultivate in people, because fear is not a sin per se.[5] But when one yields to fear, the opportunities for cowardice increase.

Many of Lewis's ideas on courage can be found in the pages of Scripture. That is where we must turn, too, if we want to understand God's perspective on how we should respond in potentially fear-inducing situations.

BIBLE HEROES AND COWARDS

The Bible is filled with accounts of real people facing tension and crisis. Both testaments show us men and women responding with different degrees of courage to such challenges. Although the situations these people faced were different from our own, they show us the abiding importance of holding on to courage with faith in God.

When giving a final charge to his successor, what did the great Israelite leader Moses say? "Maintain personal integrity"? "Rely on the counsel of godly men"? "Don't turn your back on those unruly Hebrews"? Perhaps, though no such statements are recorded. The Bible says that Moses told Joshua, "Be strong and courageous. . . . The LORD himself goes before you. . . . Do not be afraid; do not be discouraged" (Deuteronomy 31:7-8). Joshua went on to lead the conquest of Canaan in all boldness.

Although the Israelites were one people against many, they found their courage in God, and, with Him at their side, they prevailed. This is a recurring theme in Scripture, in reference both to the nation of Israel and to individuals who found courage in God. One memorable story of a courageous individual is the story of David facing Goliath (see 1 Samuel 17:32-51). Although he was a young boy, David found the courage in God to challenge the powerful warrior Goliath and was victorious. David also mentioned having fought a lion and a bear when he was a shepherd boy guarding his flock (see verses 34-37). (In the Chronicles, the boy Shasta also confronts a lion.)

Biblical courage does not necessarily mean we will be victorious in a worldly sense, but it does mean we should not waver from the truth of God despite adversity and even the possibility of death. Jesus, in this sense, offered the supreme example of courage. Despite His struggles in Gethsemane (see Matthew 26:36-46), He had the courage to go on and fulfill His destiny of suffering. Following His example, the early Christians were courageous despite the opposition they faced by way of persecution. They stood firm in their faith and heeded the words of Paul, who told them, "Keep up your courage" (Acts 27:22,25) and "Be courageous" (1 Corinthians 16:13, TNIV). During an imprisonment, Paul wrote, "Because of my chains, most of the brothers and sisters have become confident in the Lord and dare all the more to proclaim the gospel without fear" (Philippians 1:14, TNIV). And in 2 Timothy 1:7, he wrote, "God did not give us a spirit of timidity, but a spirit of power, of love and of self-discipline."

In contrast to these great virtues, cowardice is looked down upon in Scripture. For the Jewish people, and later for the Christians, cowardice indicates a lack of trust in God. In Revelation 21:8, for instance, the "cowardly" are included in a list of those whose "place will be in the fiery lake." They are grouped with "the unbelieving, the vile, the murderers, the sexually immoral, those who practice magic arts, the idolaters and all liars."

The Old Testament, too, features examples of cowardice. In Exodus when God spoke to Moses at the burning bush, Moses exhibited qualities of—if not outright—cowardice, then at least reluctance based on fear (see Exodus 3:11,13; 4:1,10,13). However, there are also instances of cowardice in military situations. In Judges 7:3, for instance, God told Gideon to reduce the number of men in the army, noting, "Anyone who trembles with fear may turn back and leave Mount Gilead." In the next sentence, we are told that twenty-two thousand men left.

The Bible contains far more examples than these cited here, but these are enough to suggest something of the diversity of the Bible's portraits of courage and cowardice. It seems the need for courage is a theme that keeps cropping up—in real life and in Narnia.

NARNIA'S BRAVEHEARTS

No one holds a monopoly on courage. But in Narnia, certain characters represent courage more clearly than do others. These characters become models for us of how to respond with bravery in the face of danger and the unknown.

Puddleglum. The marsh-wiggle Puddleglum is courageous in the sense of having fortitude as well as exhibiting bravery in battle. Always pessimistic, he nonetheless plays a valuable role in the quest to find the lost Prince Rilian in *The Silver Chair*. He bravely joins Eustace and Jill on their journey, even though he is under no obligation to do so and has not been specifically assigned the duty by Aslan. As the trio approaches Harfang (the castle of the giants), Puddleglum shows the most courage as he calls out to the porter of the giants, announcing their presence.[6] Later, Puddleglum leads a daring daylight escape from the giants, who had planned to eat them for their Autumn Feast.

In the dark castle of the Underworld, Puddleglum exhibits courage in many other ways. He boldly suggests to Eustace and Jill that they obey the fourth sign of Aslan (that they will know they have found the prince because he will be the first person to ask them to do something in Aslan's name) regardless of the consequences.[7] Shortly after freeing Rilian, they are all enchanted by the queen of Underland (she throws magical green powder on the fire in the room, plays mysterious music, and with her words attempts to convince them that Narnia and Aslan do not exist). Puddleglum challenges the queen's claims that the Overworld does not exist.[8] Then Puddleglum risks pain (his deed is described as "a very brave thing") by stamping out the enchanted fire with his bare foot, breaking the enchantment.[9] When the queen turns into a hideous serpent and attacks Rilian, Puddleglum and Eustace rush to his aid with swords drawn.

Near the end of the adventure, Jill compliments Puddleglum on his bravery by comparing him to a lion.[10] Of course, in Narnia, no mention of a lion can help conjuring up images of Aslan, the most courageous character of them all. Courage is found in unlikely places, even in a marsh-wiggle.

Shasta. A number of incidents in the story of Shasta demonstrate the courage of this peasant boy, the protagonist of *The Horse and His Boy*. It certainly took courage for Shasta to escape from his home in Calormen, though he was spurred to action by the knowledge that Arsheesh was not truly his father and that he (Shasta) would be sold into slavery. It also took courage to sneak through Tashbaan, wait alone at the ancient tombs on the other side of the city, run to warn King Lune of an impending attack, and participate in the Battle of Anvard.[11]

But the greatest example of the courage of Shasta occurs when he and his companions are being chased by a lion as they approach the home of the Hermit of the Southern March. Shasta is riding on the talking horse Bree, and the Tarkheena Aravis is riding on the talking mare Hwin. Shasta and Bree are ahead, but as Shasta glances back, he sees the lion closing in on Aravis and Hwin. Suddenly, Shasta tells Bree to stop, adding that he must go back to help. Bree (who later claims he did not hear Shasta) continues galloping wildly away from the lion. At this point, Shasta's courage clearly overrides his fear. He jumps from the horse, resulting in severe pain, and begins moving toward Aravis and Hwin. We are told that Shasta has never before behaved in such a manner and, in this instance, isn't even sure why he is responding in such a way.[12] Shasta, having grown up a peasant and the adopted son of a fisherman, likely never has had an opportunity for such courage since he rarely wanders even a short distance from his home.

Lewis, once again, was appealing to natural law. Deep down inside (to repeat a phrase often used by Lewis in the Chronicles), Shasta knows that something has to be done to help Aravis and Hwin because it is the right thing to do, even though in the end it might not do any good. Shasta is responding to a moral impulse within himself, as do we all when we are courageous in a right cause.

Reepicheep. The talking mouse Reepicheep is the epitome of courage.[13] Despite his small stature, he exhibits great valor and knightly chivalry. He fights bravely in the second Battle of Beruna against the army of Miraz and, in the process, has his tail cut off, though it is restored miraculously by Aslan (who clearly is fond of the mouse, despite Reepicheep's emphasis on honor sometimes bordering on pride).[14] In *The Voyage of the "Dawn Treader,"* when confronted with an invisible band of hostile creatures known as Duffers, Reepicheep is willing to fight them even though they cannot be seen and, therefore, may be too many to overcome. When the human crew members of the *Dawn Treader,* including King Caspian, suggest avoiding a strange darkness where Dark Island is hidden, Reepicheep urges them to go on, and, as a result, they rescue Lord Rhoop from the nightmare-inducing island. On Ramandu's Island, when the travelers encounter a mysterious banquet and are afraid to eat it, Reepicheep steps in and drinks a cup of wine from the table. Most notably, when the *Dawn Treader* reaches the end of the world, Reepicheep boldly and joyfully sails into the unknown over an enormous wall of water.[15]

Women of courage. Despite some legitimate accusations of sexism, a number of strong female characters do appear in the Chronicles.[16] These women of courage include Aravis, Jill Pole, Polly Plummer, and Lucy Pevensie.[17] In *The Horse and His Boy*, after the talking mare Hwin (courageous in her own right) convinces Aravis not to commit suicide, Aravis decides to leave her position of nobility and flee to the unknown North—a bold decision. Jill Pole exhibits courage in *The Silver Chair* when she forces herself to move on despite her claustrophobic fears in the Underworld. In

The Magician's Nephew, Polly proves a match for Digory and shows her courage by being willing to enter another world through a pool in the Wood between the Worlds.[18] But of all the courageous women of Narnia, the most brave is Lucy Pevensie.

During her reign in Narnia, Lucy is known as Queen Lucy the Valiant. Not only is Lucy valiant on the battlefield (as proved by her participation in the Battle of Anvard, for instance), she is also courageous in other situations. In *The Lion, the Witch and the Wardrobe*, she is eager to go to the aid of Tumnus the faun despite the dangers involved in undertaking such a venture. In *Prince Caspian*, when her companions refuse to believe she has seen Aslan, she is willing to go on without them in the direction to which Aslan is calling her. In *The Voyage of the "Dawn Treader,"* Lucy boldly approaches the dragon even before it is known that the beast is really Eustace. She also bravely accepts the challenge of the Duffers and alone enters the home of the mysterious magician Coriakin in order to break a spell.[19]

In Narnia, it seems, women as well as men can set a standard of courage for others.

POLTROONS IN NARNIA

Just as there are numerous inspiring examples of brave characters in the Narnia chronicles, so there are many examples of fearful characters, such as Eustace (called a "poltroon," or a contemptible coward, by Reepicheep) before his transformation. From these characters, we can learn how *not* to act.

The Duffers. When first encountered in *The Voyage of the "Dawn Treader,"* the Duffers are invisible. Although they boldly threaten the ship's landing party, they do so only because they have the clear advantage of numbers, weapons, and invisibility. They threaten to cut the throats of the newcomers if Lucy does not agree to enter the home of a magician and read a spell that will make the Duffers visible again (the spell can be uttered by only a little girl or the magician himself in order for it to work). When asked why Lucy must be the one to do this and not one of their own girls, the Duffers are forthright in stating that they are not willing to face the danger themselves. In this respect, they do not display the typical sentiment of cowardice as being shameful. It is clear, however, that they *are* cowards: They do not want to have one of their own break the spell, they are fearful of the magician Coriakin (a kindly star who is being punished by Aslan for an undisclosed incident), and they hint they are afraid of the dark—or at least of entering the magician's home in the dark.[20]

The Duffers are amusing, and it's hard to stay mad at them. But at the same time, they are clearly childish, irrational, and selfish creatures. For these reasons, and not least for their cowardice, in the end the Duffers are not creatures we should emulate.

Pittencream. A seaman aboard the *Dawn Treader,* Pittencream is mentioned only briefly. But through this character, Lewis provides another example of cowardice, one that shows just how shameful the trait is.

At this stage in the adventure, the *Dawn Treader* has reached Ramandu's Island, where the crew members find the remaining missing Narnian lords, thus fulfilling the primary purpose of their quest. In order to break the enchantment of sleep that is upon the lords, however, they are told by Ramandu that they must sail east to the end of the world and leave behind one member of their crew (Reepicheep eagerly volunteers). Nevertheless, Caspian does not feel right about asking the crew to go on after all it has been through. He explains the situation and receives a mixed response, though the seaman Rynelf gives a stirring speech about why he believes they should go on to the end of the world.[21]

In a clever psychological move, Caspian decides to present the journey to the end of the world as being a privilege rather than a request: Only the best of the crew will be allowed to continue on such a special journey. He then sends them off to consider the matter. During this time, all but three of the crew members agree to continue sailing to the end of the world. This number soon drops to one. Pittencream fears the journey to the end of the world (in other words, he fears the unknown) and yields to this fear, resulting in cowardice. Paradoxically, he also fears being left behind on Ramandu's Island, and this is what convinces him to go along with the rest. But when Caspian learns of the circumstances that have changed Pittencream's mind, he leaves him behind as a lesson.[22]

Left to his cowardice, Pittencream does not enjoy the company of Ramandu or his daughter, and neither does he much enjoy the feast that is prepared for him daily as he awaits the return of his courageous crew members. On the return journey to Narnia, Pittencream deserts the *Dawn Treader* at the Lone Islands and travels to Calormen, where he lies about his adventures by claiming he visited the end of the world. We are told that thereafter he could never endure mice — a reminder of Reepicheep's bravery in sailing to the end of the world and Pittencream's apparent disdain for the courage of the mouse.[23]

Pittencream exhibits a more common reaction to cowardice than do the Duffers in that he is seemingly ashamed of his behavior to the point of not even wanting to return to Narnia, where it will be known by everyone that his cowardice kept him from visiting the end of the world. Instead of facing up to his vice and committing himself to better behavior in the future, he decides to travel to a land where he is unknown and, by doing so, turns his cowardice into courage through dishonesty. Even though Pittencream is described as telling great tales and perhaps even lives a happy life, one cannot help but speculate that his cowardice, shame, desertion, and lies mar his moral character severely if not permanently.[24]

Uncle Andrew. In *The Magician's Nephew*, we learn how contact between Earth and Narnia is established through the fumbling magic of a character called Uncle Andrew.[25] Although Uncle Andrew is eager to pursue his studies of the occult (a bold but foolish endeavor) and is interested in learning about other worlds, he lacks the courage to explore. Instead, he first uses guinea pigs for his experiments and then deceives the young girl Polly Plummer into entering the unknown on his behalf. After Andrew's nephew, Digory, understands the situation, he tells Uncle Andrew plainly that his actions are cowardly, particularly his trickery in sending Polly into the unknown simply because Andrew is afraid to go himself. Andrew responds angrily, arguing in his defense that he is a great scholar and magician, and goes on to compare the suggestion that he be the one to participate in the experiment to sending a general to fight as a soldier.[26]

Later, when Digory and Polly return to Andrew's study with

the imposing Jadis, Andrew is initially frightened because in his experiments he never takes risks himself and is unaccustomed to facing dangers. Consequently, he is not sure what to make of Jadis's appearing before him and is soon cowering before her intimidating character. Interestingly, when Andrew is not in her presence, his vanity takes over and he begins to believe that Jadis might fall in love with him.[27]

When Andrew enters an empty world of darkness with Digory, Polly, Jadis, a cabby, and a horse, he expresses cowardly selfishness in attempting to convince Digory to abandon everyone to the empty world and leave with him. When Aslan appears and the creation of Narnia is taking place, Andrew wishes he had a gun so that he could shoot the lion — another cowardly thought, considering that the lion had done them no harm. Finally, Andrew's cowardice before the talking animals of Narnia results in his being unable to comprehend their speech or the speech of Aslan.[28] Although Andrew is eager to exploit the new world, where anything seems to grow, such as the lamppost, his cowardice and selfishness do not allow him to see reality clearly.

At the end of the story, we are told that Andrew goes to live with Digory and his family. Andrew no longer dabbles in magic and apparently becomes a better person.[29]

We, too, can learn a lesson — the lesson about courage that Narnia's bravehearts and poltroons have to teach us. Life is like a fairy tale in that as we walk along life's trail, we encounter fearful challenges. How will we react — with courage and faith in God, or with fear and cowardice? Our response has much to do with the destination we will eventually come to.

COURAGE THIS SIDE OF THE WARDROBE

While few of us are soldiers who know what it is like to fight on a real battlefield, our everyday experiences provide opportunities for courage on the battlefield of life. We may not be called to face a life-and-death situation, but each day, if we are on the alert, we will find opportunities for courage or cowardice. In the marketplace, at home, at church, wherever we are, situations both mundane and dramatic will call on our resources of courage to do what is right.

Indeed, defending the very principle of right and wrong requires courage today. In a world of increasing moral relativism, Christians must stand for objective moral truth and see opportunities for courage as opportunities for character development. As J. P. Moreland observed, "The Christian mind requires the courage to face the truth and to stand up for it even when doing so is not popular. Bravery does not imply the absence of fear, but the ability to rise above and not be controlled by it."[30]

When the Duffers display their cowardice by refusing to read the spell that would make them visible, they allow Lucy the opportunity to display courage by doing it in their stead. Like Lucy, we, too, may encounter vice or various forms of moral evil, but its very existence allows us the opportunity to exhibit virtue. When good is missing and evil results, we must fill the vacuum of virtue with good.

The decisions we make in response to challenges in life will shape our character for better or for worse. But how, exactly, can one develop a character of courage? There are, of course, instances when natural law at work within us will take over instinctively and courage will result, perhaps unexpectedly, such as when Shasta jumps off Bree in order to intervene during the lion attack on Aravis and Hwin. But what about developing courage as a response to everyday challenges, particularly trying times, or other situations? One cannot merely read about courage and expect to become courageous. As noted earlier, the Bible offers insights on courage, including the observation that courage is tied to faith in God and His character (see Deuteronomy 31:6; Joshua 1:9; 1 Chronicles 28:20; Acts 27:25). Therefore, part of developing the virtue of courage involves faith in God based on the knowledge that He is with us even when life presents us with challenges.

One way to develop courage based on Narnian insights is to follow the example of Reepicheep. The talking mouse possesses courage in battle as well as courage to face the unknown. He is willing to sail to the end of the world on his own if need be. If his coracle sinks, he will swim. If he begins to drown, he is willing to die with dignity.[31] Moreover, the mouse's faith in Aslan is clear and unwavering. Reepicheep understands at some level that his earthly life is a mere training ground or precursor to eternity, so why not be courageous for the sake of Aslan? Reepicheep represents an idealistic sort of courage that we can strive for but that will require effort to cultivate.

The alternative—namely cowardice—brings with it no redeeming qualities. It is a vice that cannot be enjoyed but only endured.

Reflection and Response Questions

1. Think about the discussion in *The Voyage of the "Dawn Treader"* about whether the ship should continue eastward to the end of the world. This is the conversation in which Reepicheep states that if the *Dawn Treader* fails, he will paddle on in his coracle; and if the coracle sinks, he will swim; and if he can swim no longer, he will sink with his nose toward the sunrise. What is one time in your life when you acted courageously? What is one time when you acted cowardly?

2. What choice or situation lying ahead of you right now worries you? Setting aside your *feelings* about the matter for the moment, what is the *right* thing for you to do in that choice or situation? Pray for the courage to do what is right and for God's help to develop a pattern of courage in your life.

Chapter 3

Fairness *and* Unfairness

In *The Lion, the Witch and the Wardrobe*, the White Witch demands justice because of the traitorous actions of Edmund Pevensie. In *The Voyage of the "Dawn Treader,"* after the slave trade is abolished, two Calormenes request reimbursement for their purchases. Caspian acknowledges their request as fair. In the same book, Eustace, who believes he was judged wrongly, notes in his journal that he believes he was treated unfairly. In *The Silver Chair*, a reformed Eustace asks Jill if her reaction to him is fair when he is defending his improved behavior. Later Jill apologizes, admitting her reaction was unfair. Shasta considers the behavior of Aravis unfair, in *The Horse and His Boy*, after hearing that Aravis drugged a girl as part of a plan to escape an arranged marriage. Andrew Ketterley, in *The Magician's Nephew*, complains that his situation is unfair (he is shaken after accidentally being pulled into another world). In *The Last Battle*, Shift the ape claims it is naturally fair that he should get to eat the best food brought by Puzzle the donkey. Later, Shift implores Puzzle to be fair when Shift is trying to convince him to do something very wrong.[1]

All of these characters, both good and bad, are calling upon some sort of standard by which fairness and unfairness must be judged. The witch appeals to Deep Magic, making a true claim, but her purposes are evil. Caspian agrees that money paid for freed slaves must be returned. Eustace, who was clearly attempting to steal water but was caught by Reepicheep, complains that he was treated unfairly. In *The Silver Chair*, Eustace is really in a position to appeal to fairness and does so, convincing Jill by offering evidence of his changed moral character. Shasta, who is later proven correct, is concerned about the way Aravis treated a girl by drugging her. Andrew, shocked by the events of the day, laments his predicament but does not acknowledge that he is at fault, though he clearly is responsible. Shift the ape routinely convinces Puzzle to do what he wants by appealing to standards he himself fails to follow (Shift cares about fairness only insofar as it benefits him).

This sort of reasoning is exactly what C. S. Lewis wrote about in several of his works, including *Mere Christianity* and *Miracles*. In *Mere Christianity*, Lewis began his case for the existence of ultimate right and wrong by noting that we have all witnessed people arguing. When they do, they appeal to some kind of standard of justice.[2] Children as well as adults know when something is not fair, and the purpose of arguing is to determine who is right and who is wrong. In *Miracles*, Lewis notes that even naturalists who claim to deny objective standards of right and wrong, or good and evil, are inconsistent. When they encounter injustice, they cast aside their naturalism and behave as they ought; that is, they at least for a time behave as though such standards do in fact exist. Lewis wrote that this happens simply because of our humanity, which includes elements of God's glory. Despite efforts to deny God and His standards, since we are human beings, we must behave accordingly.[3]

When we sense that we have been ill treated, we call for fairness. When we want something that perhaps we don't deserve, however, we may try to bend the quality of fairness for our own benefit. Whether it's who gets promoted at work, what kinds of punishments are meted out for wrongdoing, how the government should allocate its social service monies, or any of countless other circumstances in which people have competing claims, fairness and unfairness are eminently practical subjects. A sound understanding of these qualities can guide us daily in our relations with each other.

FAIRNESS: THE NEW NAME FOR JUSTICE

Everyone seems to grasp the concept of fairness, but when pressed, they find it difficult to define. *Fairness* means "justice."[4] But what is justice? A dictionary of ethics defines *justice* as "a virtue characterized by the rendering of what is due or merited, fairness and impartiality."[5] We naturally think of the legal system as an effort to be fair and just. But Lewis recognized there is more to justice than what is found in courts. Lewis considered justice an older term for fairness, and as one of the cardinal virtues, justice holds a special place because it must include a number of other virtues within it (such as honesty and the commitment to stick to promises).[6]

Lewis was correct in acknowledging that justice is more than what we seek in courts. In fact, philosophical studies of the term generally divide justice into three categories. *Distributive justice* addresses matters of fairness in relation to sharing in communities. *Remedial justice* seeks to correct unjust behavior, as in a court system. *Retributive justice* pursues retribution — that is, doing as much as possible to make right what was wrong. All three forms of justice are present in the Chronicles.

Are *unfairness* and *injustice* merely the opposites of *fairness* and *justice*? In some ways the answer is yes. If evil is a parasite, perverting and spoiling good (as Lewis argued), then injustice and unfairness may be viewed as occurring when justice and fairness are lacking. "Want of equity" is a phrase appearing in the definition of injustice in one dictionary.[7] Based on Lewis's insights into justice, he would view injustice as resulting from a lack of virtue. This naturally fits with his perspective of evil as a privation.

Recall, too, that when Lewis was an atheist, he argued against God on the basis of what he saw as a cruel and unjust universe. What puzzled him, however, was how he got the idea of injustice in the first place. Despite his line of argumentation intended to disprove God, he found that he was obliged to acknowledge that his concept of justice was completely sensible.[8] In short, the rational basis for calling something unjust must rest upon the existence of a real standard of justice, which Lewis argued flows from God.

We see justice by precept and by example in the Bible. God embodies fairness and justice, and His people are called to be fair and just in emulation of Him.

The Golden Rules of Narnia

The Bible speaks more to justice and injustice than specifically to fairness and unfairness. Nevertheless, the Golden Rule, as spoken by Christ, certainly appeals to fairness: "In everything, do to others what you would have them do to you, for this sums up the Law and the Prophets" (Matthew 7:12). As we would like to be treated with fairness and justice, likewise we should strive to treat others in such a way.

Although much of the biblical material regarding justice concerns divine justice, other aspects of justice are also included, such as the example of distributive justice in Acts 4:32: "All the believers were one in heart and mind. No one claimed that any of his possessions was his own, but they shared everything they had." The Golden Rules of Narnia also seek to satisfy the biblical Golden Rule as well as emphasize concepts of sharing and, in turn, fairness in the sense of equity.

Biblically, divine justice is not as closely identified with fairness as it is in normal English parlance. Instead, divine justice is concerned with what is right, or righteousness. As a result, God's justice and His righteousness are often associated in the Bible, such as in Psalm 89:14, 103:6, Isaiah 5:16, Jeremiah 9:24, and Hosea 2:19. The Messiah will establish and uphold His kingdom "with justice and righteousness" (Isaiah 9:7). Divine justice is also associated with judgment. But God is not vindictive in judgment; indeed, He is merciful. Justice is, in fact, an aspect of His holiness. A holy God cannot accept injustice.

But the story of Christianity is more than a story of the righteous judgment of the Lord; it is also a story of redemption—that of offering Jesus as an atonement for human fallenness (something touched upon by Lewis in the Chronicles, most dramatically in *The Lion, the Witch and the Wardrobe*). Through Jesus, God satisfies the requirements of divine justice for us, not because of what we have done or can do but because of what Christ has done and will do in us.

Human justice is fallible, but God still calls His followers to strive for justice and avoid perversions of justice. Many Old Testament passages speak against denying or depriving justice (see Exodus 23:6; Proverbs 18:5; Isaiah 10:1; 29:21; Amos 2:7; Malachi 3:5) and against perverting justice (see Exodus 23:2; Leviticus 19:15; Deuteronomy 16:19). This is to be expected in light of the Old Testament emphasis on obeying God's laws. Kings and governments as a whole should also value justice (see 1 Kings 10:9; Ezra 7:25; Psalms 72:1; 99:4; Proverbs 16:10). In 1 Kings 3:11, the Lord is pleased with Solomon for asking for "discernment in administering justice," while Proverbs 29:4 reads, "By justice a king gives a country stability." As Isaiah 1:16-17 puts it,

> Stop doing wrong,
>   learn to do right!
> Seek justice,
>   encourage the oppressed.

The theme of justice for all, particularly for foreigners ("aliens") and the oppressed or the poor, recurs throughout the Old Testament (see Deuteronomy 24:17; Ezekiel 22:29; Amos 2:7; 5:12). Psalm 106:3 emphasizes the importance of justice as a way of life and a part of one's character:

Blessed are they who maintain justice,
who constantly do what is right.

A virtuous person, who has cultivated such things as justice, is more likely to make the right decision in a given circumstance than someone who does not value or develop virtue. "Evil men do not understand justice" (Proverbs 28:5).

While the New Testament offers grace to those under law, it by no means minimizes the importance of law and justice. In Matthew 23:23, for example, Jesus chastises "teachers of the law and Pharisees" because they have "neglected the more important matters of the law — justice, mercy and faithfulness." Moreover, as Paul declared, one day God will "judge the world with justice" through Christ (Acts 17:31). The New Testament also notes examples of injustice, such as when referring to Isaiah 53:7-8 in Acts 8:32-33, a passage referring to Christ: "In his humiliation he was deprived of justice."

Biblical themes related to fairness and unfairness find creative expression in the Chronicles of Narnia. Characters who display exemplary fairness, for example, provide a model for us to follow.

THE DEEPER MAGIC OF JUSTICE

Characters in the Chronicles speak a lot about justice and fairness, and sometimes they even behave with wonderful fairness toward each other. These characters include (at times) the Pevensie children and several more. But among them all, Aslan must come first.

Because Aslan is essentially a Christ figure, his actions are examples of divine justice. As such, his justice is best described not as fairness in the sense of being equitable but as righteousness. He comes to set things right, as Mr. Beaver says when quoting a rhyme.[9]

Aslan, justice, and Deep Magic. The terms *Deep Magic* and *Deeper Magic* are significant in *The Lion, the Witch and the Wardrobe.* Deep Magic is first mentioned by the White Witch in relation to her claim of a right to sacrifice Edmund for his treachery.[10] From the witch we learn that the Deep Magic can be traced to the beginning of Narnia and that the words of the Deep Magic are written in three places: the Table of Stone, the fire-stones of the Secret Hill, and the scepter of the Emperor-beyond-the-Sea.[11] If the Deep Magic is not satisfied, Narnia will be destroyed.[12] Aslan confirms that the witch's account of the Deep Magic is true and speaks privately with her. After the discussion, Aslan announces that the witch has renounced her claim on Edmund's life. In the following chapter of *The Lion, the Witch and the Wardrobe*, we learn that Aslan has offered to satisfy the justice of the Deep Magic by willingly taking the place of Edmund and is sacrificed by the witch at the Stone Table (this is discussed further in chapter 5 of this book).

Susan and Lucy witness the horrible event and are heartbroken. They hear a loud noise, realize the Stone Table has broken and the body of Aslan is gone, and wonder if more magic is at work. Aslan appears, larger than they remembered him, and affirms that more magic is indeed at work. But it is Deeper Magic from before the dawn of time. This Deeper Magic states that if someone who is innocent volunteers to take the place of a traitor and be sacrificed, the Stone Table would break and the innocent one sacrificed would come back to life.[13] Deeper Magic, then, appears to refer to eternal justice entailing a special kind of sacrifice.

The story has parallels to the Christian account of Jesus fulfilling the just demands of the Law by His willing sacrifice for sinful humanity, thereby providing atonement. Aslan demonstrates this divine and eternal justice. Although in the immediate context, Aslan's death is only for Edmund, as the Chronicles develop, Lewis hints that Aslan's sacrifice applies to all of Narnia—or at least extends beyond Edmund.[14]

Fairness and children. Throughout the Chronicles, Lewis included examples of fairness among children. They are not exempt from natural law, and Lewis referred to children in his argument in *Mere Christianity*, observing that adults as well as children appeal to the law of human nature.[15] The examples of fairness involving children in the Chronicles are of a different sort than the justice of Aslan. In these instances, Lewis was not focusing on divine justice but on fairness or equity. As such, they are often examples of distributive justice within a small group. However, there are also examples of retributive justice among children, such as the end of *The Silver Chair*, when the bullies of Experiment House (a school) are taught a lesson by Eustace, Jill, and Caspian.[16]

Prince Caspian offers an excellent example of distributive justice when Peter, Susan, Edmund, and Lucy are pulled from a railway station, where they are awaiting their return to school, and into Narnia. After the initial joy of realizing that they may be in Narnia and will not have to go back to school anytime soon, the practical Susan observes that soon they will want to eat and will consequently need to plan something. Unfortunately, Lucy and Susan do not have their lunches. After exploring a while and finding a stream to drink from, the children again turn to the question of food. Susan suggests that perhaps they should save the two lunches for a time of more dire hunger, while Lucy remarks that now that they have had a good drink, it would be nice if they could also have their fill of food. Edmund notes that in the heat the sandwiches will soon go bad. In the end, they decide to divide the lunches equally among themselves, even though it isn't enough to make a decent meal for any of them.[17]

This is fairness. The Edmund of *The Lion, the Witch and the Wardrobe* would have scoffed at the idea of dividing the sandwiches equally, instead wanting his sandwich all to himself. But the children now know enough about fairness to equally divide the food. In this instance, fairness does not mean that everyone gets enough to be satisfied, only that everyone gets a fair share.

Another example of fairness among the children occurs later in *Prince Caspian*, when Lucy claims to have seen Aslan but no one else has. Peter questions whether Lucy really means she saw Aslan, while Susan goes a step further with her skepticism by casting doubt on what Lucy may have seen. Lucy affirms that she, in fact, did see Aslan, specifies where, and declares that it is a sign as to the direction they should take. At this point, Lucy is near tears. She is in a situation similar to that in which she found herself when she claimed to have visited another world via a wardrobe early in *The Lion, the Witch and the Wardrobe*. No one would believe her then, and it appears no one will believe her now. Edmund points out that Lucy was right in the previous instance and says that based on her past record, it would be fair to believe her in the current situation.[18] In the end, however, a vote is taken, and Lucy, overruled and feeling rejected, follows the party weeping.

In this instance, an effort to be fair is made, but the decision is not in the hands of one person alone. Still, Edmund makes a reasonable point, and despite the opposition from Peter, Susan, and Trumpkin the dwarf, he sticks to what he believes to be a fair decision — to believe Lucy. But fairness is not always determined by numbers.

Justice and the murder of the Dryads. In *The Last Battle,* we learn how, under the pretense of orders from Aslan, men from Calormen have entered Narnia and are cutting down trees that have living spirits (Dryads) in them. Moreover, the soldiers are whipping horses as the animals are working hard to pull the fallen trees. King Tirian and his unicorn friend Jewel first hear of this situation from a Dryad who has traveled to the king to cry out for justice and protection.[19] Tirian is shocked at the injustice. He leaps to his feet and draws his sword. Then, in a dramatic and touching scene, the Dryad falls over and dies because her tree has been cut down.

Tirian, still grieving over the loss of the Dryad, is angry. Despite the warnings of Roonwit the centaur for them to be careful of their anger even though they are reacting to a real injustice, Tirian and Jewel respond rashly.[20] They rush to the site where trees are being felled and are further outraged to see the sacred forest being chopped down and horses being whipped. When he realizes these are talking horses, Tirian is further enraged by the cruelty of the Calormenes. In response, Tirian and Jewel kill two Calormenes.

This is an example of retributive justice gone wrong. It is true that justice should be done—the killing of the Dryads and the mistreatment of the horses must be stopped—but the manner in which it is attempted results in injustice. Shortly after the bloody incident, Tirian acknowledges he was in the wrong to attack two unarmed Calormenes and knows he must be brought to Aslan for judgment.[21]

The example of Tirian shows that injustice is all too easy to commit, even when one wants to do the right thing. Other characters in the Chronicles show us more plainly what unfairness or injustice can look like.

TARNISHING THE GOLDEN RULE

There are a number of examples of injustice in the Chronicles. In fact, there are far more examples than one would need to illustrate the trait (just as there are in our own world, sadly).

Slavery and the Lone Islands. For hundreds of years, the Lone Islands (ostensibly under the rule of Narnia) have been neglected until King Caspian arrives with his crew, in *The Voyage of the "Dawn Treader."* After Caspian, Edmund, Eustace, Lucy, and Reepicheep are captured while visiting one of the islands, they quickly learn of the existence of a slave trade in the region, sanctioned by Governor Gumpas. As Paul Ford correctly observed, "Gumpas is the epitome of the petty civil servant, immersed in detail and unmindful of the larger issues."[22] When he is confronted by an outraged Caspian who speaks vehemently against the slave trade, Gumpas claims he had no choice because slavery is an economic necessity to the Lone Islands. He is a bureaucrat who substantiates his actions by charts and data rather than justice.[23]

Gumpas views slavery as an important aspect of progress for his realm. Caspian, however, sees clearly that slavery is wrong. He does not view the slave trade as benefiting Narnia by bringing in goods, but even if it did, Caspian boldly declares that the trade must end. Because he has arrived with only a small company of men and a ploy devised to make Gumpas think that Caspian has more ships at his disposal, the king is taking quite a risk. Taking an even greater risk, he relieves Governor Gumpas of his position and appoints the Lord Bern as Duke of the Lone Islands. Caspian then rides to the slave market in order to find and release his captive friends and announce the end of the slave trade. When two Calormene merchants indicate they would like their money back for their slave purchases, Caspian sees the fairness in their request and grants it to them as well as to anyone who had purchased a slave that day.[24]

The Calormen Empire. Calormen is presented in a largely negative light in the Chronicles.[25] It is important to stress, however, that Lewis did not view Calormen as all bad. In fact, when in Aslan's country, Lucy can see that the great city of Tashbaan, described in *The Horse and His Boy* as one of the wonders of the world, is preserved in Aslan's country.[26] This must mean Lewis believed there was some good in Calormen culture, because elements of their great city are preserved by Aslan. Perhaps Lewis had in mind the Calormen love for storytelling, their architecture, and the beauty of their gardens. Nevertheless, in the fairy-tale world of Narnia, the Calormen Empire is a clear example of injustice.

One example of the empire's injustice is its attitude toward human life. The caste system of the culture leaves little room for fairness and justice. The only rule on the crowded streets of Tashbaan is that those who are lesser in status must make way for those who are greater.[27] This concept is clearly at odds with the Christian sentiment of fairness and equal treatment, as seen in passages such as James 2:1-9, which warns against showing favoritism. The Calormene nobility lead pampered lives, while nearly everyone else is consigned to the difficult life of a peasant. Slavery is common. Calormene women "are chattels of their husbands and parents. Their marriages are arranged and their own feelings are immaterial."[28] The empire is warlike and eager to expand. Prince Rabadash's desire to take Archenland and then attack Narnia typifies the warlike behavior and rashness of the empire (see chapter 6). Additionally, the leader of Calormen, known as the Tisroc, cares little for human life, as shown by his having three cooks executed because food they prepared gave him indigestion.[29] The Calormene are a proud race, and their excessive pride leads to injustice.

The justice of Narnia presents a sharp contrast to typical behavior in Calormen. Narnian women have many more rights and are in general liberated. Women in Narnia are allowed to fight in battles, such as when Queen Lucy fights at the Battle of Anvard in *The Horse and His Boy*, and marriage is not forced upon women. Slavery in Narnia is also unheard of, which is why Caspian has such a strong revulsion to it. Even "dumb" animals of Narnia are treated with respect and not as creatures to be abused. Narnia appears to fight only in just wars, protecting its borders or fighting for a worthy cause, such as that against the White Witch and her army (see chapter 6). Unlike the Calormene, Narnians highly value life of all kinds, but they will fight to the death when the cause is just.

False appeals to fairness. In *The Last Battle*, despite Shift the ape's self-centeredness leaving little room for fairness as traditionally defined, he appeals to it anyway in order to get his way. This is most evident in his dealings with Puzzle the donkey, who is more slave than friend. Puzzle is a simple animal, too often admitting as much and not often enough taking responsibility for his behavior, and he is easily manipulated by Shift (see chapter 4). Even though Puzzle does all the work, including traveling to town to get food, Shift takes the best foods that Puzzle returns with and doesn't share them. Shift claims this arrangement is only fair since an ape is unable to eat grass and thistles.[30]

In another instance, Shift is trying to convince Puzzle to do something that is clearly wrong, but when the donkey protests, Shift points out Puzzle's alleged lack of intelligence and then offers to do the thinking for Puzzle. The ape then has the audacity to say, "Why don't you treat me as I treat you?" falsely appealing to the Golden Rule for the sake of his own gain.[31] (Of course, if Puzzle really treated Shift in the same manner, the arrangement would hardly be acceptable to Shift.) The discussion reaches its peak when Shift tells Puzzle to be fair.[32] It is not fairness or justice that Shift is seeking. Instead, he wants his own way and finds that a false appeal to fairness will add enough truth to his argument to get him what he wants.

The story of Shift reminds us of how we don't like to see false appeals to fairness by others around us. It should also remind us of the importance of seeking to act fairly and justly ourselves. God, by His Spirit, aids those who genuinely want to do what is right.

GRABBING THE INITIATIVE

Everyone wants to be treated fairly. Lewis argued that it is human nature to desire fairness, because it is based on the inescapability of natural law. Every now and then, he notes in *Mere Christianity*, we may come across a person who does not conform to natural law, but that does not negate its existence.[33] A recurring phrase in the Chronicles, "deep down inside," was used by Lewis to capture natural law at work in the hearts of individuals, for the law is "written" on the heart (see Romans 2:14-15).[34] When we feel the pangs of justice deep down inside — pangs that conform to God's revelation — we must, like Caspian, take action to right the wrongs around us.

Sometimes standing up for justice may result in our looking foolish in the eyes of others, being persecuted for our beliefs, or feeling as though we are fighting a losing battle in the face of marked and extensive opposition. Justice, however, is not determined by numbers but by God and His standards. When true Christians living and breathing true Christianity are seemingly the lone voice in opposition to questionable behavior in culture, that is usually when they are most correct in their assessment of and response to injustice. But that does not make the task easy; it only makes it right. Athanasius struggled so much throughout his life against heresy that his actions gave rise to the phrase "Athanasius *contra mundo*," meaning "Athanasius against the world."[35] To be *contra mundo* for the sake of justice is a divine command.

Justice encompasses a number of other ethical traits, including courage, honesty, humility, and mercy.[36] We must, however, proceed carefully as well as prayerfully when seeking to right what is wrong. There is a place for righteous Christian anger in the face of injustice, but such anger should not spur us to commit further acts of injustice by behaving rashly as Tirian and Jewel did when confronted with outrageous and abusive behavior.

We must also realize that perfect justice in an imperfect world will always elude our best efforts. Only God's justice, mirrored in Aslan, is perfect. And yet it is the injustices of our "groaning" world (Romans 8:22) that in a strange way grant us the opportunity for justice — the opportunity to be light in the darkness (see Matthew 5:14-16). Returning to the concept of evil as a privation, injustice exists where the good that should be there (justice) is missing. Christians are called to stand up for justice and denounce injustice.

As noted earlier in this chapter, the Golden Rule appeals to our sense of fairness. Eugene Peterson offers the following rendition of the famous saying of Christ: "Here is a simple, rule-of-thumb guide for behavior: Ask yourself what you want people to do for you, then grab the initiative and do it for *them*. Add up God's Law and Prophets and this is what you get" (Matthew 7:12, MSG). A key to cultivating fairness in our lives is remembering the Golden Rule. We must make a conscious effort (that is, "grab the initiative," as Peterson puts it) to place ourselves in someone else's position and apply the simple yet profound maxim of "do to others what you would have them do to you" in everyday situations.

Of course, the Golden Rule is not a magic formula for creating virtue in our lives. Certainly, it is important to know it, but we must also combine it with our love for God and desire to serve Him—characteristics that flow from discipleship and spiritual growth. We are sensitive to being treated unfairly because we know deep down inside that there is a standard for justice and injustice. But we must extend our sensitivity to this standard beyond ourselves and apply it to others. If we do this within the context of the Golden Rule, we can rest assured that we have taken an important step in treating others fairly.

Reflection and Response Questions

1. Thinking about fairness and unfairness, which of the following Narnian characters do you identify with the most?

    - Eustace in his early days on the *Dawn Treader* (because you felt you were treated unfairly when you didn't get what you wanted)?

    - The four Pevensie children with only two lunches between them (because you wanted to share equally with others)?

    - Tirian and Jewel avenging the Dryads' murder (because you went too far in the pursuit of justice or fairness)?

2. Search your conscience. Is there a time recently that you may have treated someone unfairly? If so, plan how you will apologize and make amends.

CHAPTER 4

HONESTY *and* DISHONESTY

In *The Last Battle*, we are introduced to an old talking ape named Shift, whose name is appropriate to his character: He is shifty and exhibits numerous vices, such as greed, gluttony, sloth, selfishness, and dishonesty. One day as Shift is walking near Caldron Pool with Puzzle the donkey, he notices something in the water. After convincing Puzzle to retrieve the item, Shift realizes that it is a lion's skin. Shift quickly hatches a plan. He convinces Puzzle to wear the skin and trick Narnians into thinking Aslan has come. The ape means to use Puzzle and the lion's skin for his own gain or, as he puts it, to fix what is wrong.[1] To Shift, this primarily means more food and drink for himself without having to expend any effort on his part. In this way — through blatant dishonesty — Shift plans to satisfy his every need and desire. And the shocking thing is, the plan actually works — at least for a time. Narnia is deceived.

C. S. Lewis had much to say on the topics of honesty and dishonesty in the Chronicles of Narnia. For the careful reader, Lewis's advice is both practical and relevant. Each of us faces choices every day in life where we could either tell the truth or tell a lie. This is so in the marketplace, in school, at home — everywhere, in short, where we have to deal with other people. And sometimes telling a lie seems like an easier, more comfortable, or more advantageous option. That's why we need to develop a character of honesty so that when a choice arises, we don't even have to think about it. We will tell the truth.

Pontius Pilate probably was being rhetorical when he asked, "What is truth?" (Many relativists today could relate to him.) But for us, the first step toward a character marked by honesty is genuinely delving into the meaning of *truth* and *honesty* versus *lies* and *dishonesty*.

To Tell the Truth

Theologians, philosophers, and great thinkers (C. S. Lewis among them) have pondered deeply the qualities of honesty and dishonesty. What are they? How are they expressed? What do they mean?

While honesty may be viewed as an aspect of fairness and justice, it is distinguished by the qualities of sincerity and truthfulness. R. E. O. White notes that honesty means "truthfulness, openness, avoidance of deceit, either in practical affairs or in personal character."[2] Honesty may also be said to relate to "pursuing truth (intellectual honesty)" as well as "being truthful in relationships with others (moral honesty)."[3] In the Chronicles of Narnia, moral honesty is most evident. The concept of truth in relation to honesty is also important, as honesty presupposes that absolute truth exists and that one ought to be true to it (Lewis held to the correspondence view of truth, which asserts that truth is that which corresponds to reality).[4] We must also strive to be honest with ourselves as well as with those around us.

Lewis wrote that we can be deceived only if a proposition has affinities to reality, adding that we cannot be deceived unless someone convinces us that he or she is being honest.[5] He goes on, by way of example, to make the distinction that fantasy literature is not deceptive, noting that fairy tales do not deceive and neither are we deceived by reading science fiction or classics such as *Beowulf* or Homer's *Odyssey*. We know they are imagined works. There is a greater danger, said Lewis, in being deceived by other kinds of writing, such as novels or articles in popular magazines, that seek to communicate a particular worldview relating to subjects such as ethics, religion, and sociology.[6] Such writings may deceive us because they are false, even if the intent of the author may not necessarily be deception.

Most notably, dishonesty includes deliberate forms of deception, such as lying or other forms of trickery intended to mask the truth. To mislead by withholding information may also be viewed as being dishonest, but even Christian ethicists admit that not all such situations in a fallen world are clear-cut. One dictionary defines dishonesty in part as "lack of probity or integrity," with *probity* referring to "moral excellence."[7] References to defrauding and stealing are also used in some dictionaries. Applying the concept of evil as privation, when the good is absent (honesty), an opportunity is given for evil (dishonesty) to proliferate in a parasitical sense. We may, then, conclude that dishonesty exists when truth is robbed by dishonesty. In addition to being dishonest in relation to others, one may also be dishonest to oneself by acts of self-deception, such as in the case of Edmund in *The Lion, the Witch and the Wardrobe*. He knows within himself that the White Witch is evil, but he deceives himself into thinking otherwise because of his feeling of greed and desire for revenge.[8]

Our concepts of honesty and dishonesty are best clarified by looking at what God has to say about them in His Word.

Honest (and Dishonest) to God

The Bible values honesty and condemns dishonesty. It tells us that God Himself is — among other things — holy, just, and true; that is, truth is rooted in His character, and, therefore, we should seek to emulate His truthfulness by acting honestly and avoiding dishonesty. Moreover, as R. E. O. White adds, other biblical motivations for honesty "are the law of love (Rom. 13:9-10; I Cor. 6:8; Eph. 4:15) and Christian unity, which dishonesty destroys (Eph. 4:25-28; cf. Col. 3:9)."[9]

Several biblical passages address honesty and dishonesty. The ninth commandment reads, "You shall not give false testimony against your neighbor" (Exodus 20:16), thus supporting the value of truth. Other passages, such as Leviticus 19:11, reiterate this ("Do not steal. Do not lie. Do not deceive one another"), while Proverbs 12:22 warns, "The LORD detests lying lips." The New Testament, too, urges Christians to avoid dishonesty: "Each of you must put off falsehood and speak truthfully to his neighbor" (Ephesians 4:25). Christ, being God in the flesh, is the embodiment of truth (see John 14:6).

While the Bible is clearly against dishonesty, the question is invariably raised regarding Rahab the harlot in the Old Testament book of Joshua. Rahab hid two Hebrew spies on the roof of her home, and when confronted with a message from the king of Jericho, replied in part, "The men left. I don't know which way they went. Go after them quickly. You may catch up with them" (Joshua 2:5). Two New Testament passages are sometimes cited as approving of Rahab's lie: Hebrews 11:31 and James 2:25. But a careful examination of these passages reveals that Rahab is never praised specifically for lying. Her boldness of faith is commended, not her lie.

Still, some have made allowance for Rahab because of her difficult situation. Old Testament scholar Gleason Archer observed, "In Rahab's case there were special circumstances that operated in her favor . . . the lie meant for her a step of faith that put her very life in jeopardy." Archer went on to note that the "safer thing for her to do" would have been to tell the truth.[10] Instead she was willing to risk her own life because of her faith in the God of Israel.

When values appear to conflict, such as telling the truth or lying in a difficult situation, Christian ethics offers various perspectives. One option is to claim that there is no conflict and state that the only Christian solution is to tell the truth and trust in God for the outcome. A second approach admits that an ethical conflict exists and that lying is always wrong but suggests that it is better to choose the lesser evil. A third option does not view lying in a difficult situation as a lesser evil but rather as a greater good. Thus, if someone knocks on your door with the intent to do harm to people in your home (such as shooting them with a gun), the greater good is to lie about their presence in order to save their lives.[11]

These examples are enough to show that honesty is not always a simple matter and that the Bible strongly promotes honesty as a virtue.

RISK TAKERS FOR THE TRUTH

The same kinds of dilemmas about telling the truth that we face in our daily lives appear in the Chronicles of Narnia as well. Some Narnian characters have the sort of nature that leads them to lie, and we'll get to these negative examples shortly. Other characters, however, show us what it means to have the courage to tell the truth. Among these are central character Lucy Pevensie, a group of feasting animals, and the tutor Doctor Cornelius.

Lucy Pevensie. Lucy is consistently honest throughout the Chronicles. Not surprisingly, she is one of the most well-developed characters in the series and the human most attuned to the presence of Aslan. Lucy is willing to tell the truth even in situations where honesty results in emotional pain and suffering for her. In *The Lion, the Witch and the Wardrobe*, after she explains to her siblings that she has visited another world through the wardrobe, her brother Peter thinks she is joking. Lucy responds honestly, claiming that she is not trying to trick them. She begins to cry because they do not believe her. As the narrator explains, although Lucy could easily have been reconciled to the others by agreeing that she made up the account, she refused to do so because she was an honest child.[12] Despite her siblings disbelieving her, and Edmund, in particular, teasing her, Lucy clings to the truth.[13]

Lucy is honest with herself and with others. She rarely conceals her true feelings, except when they might embarrass another, such as when she longs to pick up the valiant mouse Reepicheep and hug him.[14] In general, however, she honestly expresses how she feels and is forthright.

The feasting animals. Honesty is clearly valued in Narnia, as exhibited by a group of feasting animals in *The Lion, the Witch and the Wardrobe*. The fading winter of the White Witch has resulted in the entry of Father Christmas into Narnia. In addition to giving special gifts to Peter, Susan, and Lucy, Father Christmas provides a feast for a group of talking animals; the group consists of two squirrels and their children, a dwarf, a fox, and two satyrs. When the witch comes across the group of creatures, she is outraged and asks where the feast came from. The fox honestly replies that the feast was a gift. When pressed further, the fox stammers and says that the feast was provided by Father Christmas. At this point, the witch is even angrier. In her rage, she hypocritically accuses the animals of a number of vices: gluttony, waste, and self-indulgence. She jumps from her sledge and approaches the animals menacingly, offering them a chance to admit they are lying so that they might be forgiven. Despite the animals' fright, a young squirrel, obviously worked up over the encounter, squeaks emphatically that Father Christmas has indeed provided the feast. The witch then turns all the feasting animals to stone. Their honesty is repaid with cruelty.[15]

Doctor Cornelius. In *Prince Caspian*, Doctor Cornelius becomes Caspian's tutor, replacing the nurse who was removed from her position for telling Caspian stories of Old Narnia (King Miraz,

Caspian's uncle, does not approve of such stories). Caspian anticipates that he will hate his new tutor, but he is quickly taken by him. Cornelius is an honest educator and values truth.[16] As such, even though he knows the potential danger to himself, he tells Caspian more stories of Old Narnia, confirming the fantastic tales the boy has heard.[17] At great personal risk, Cornelius goes on to relate to Caspian the history of how the Telmarines overthrew Old Narnia by violence and are now attempting to erase the memory of it.

Although Cornelius keeps his nature as a half-dwarf to himself, he is not overtly dishonest about it. Considering his overall character, it is likely that if asked directly about his heritage, he would tell the truth. But taking into account the hostile nature of the political climate he is in, he opts for self-preservation and passes himself off as a small old man. His silence is nothing like some of the true acts of dishonesty we see in the Chronicles.

MASKS OF DECEIT

The honest characters in the Chronicles of Narnia share pages with numerous dishonest ones. Lying, cheating, and deceiving are typical practices among the most reprehensible characters to infest Narnia.

The giants of Harfang. When the queen of Underland first encounters Eustace, Jill, and Puddleglum the marsh-wiggle in *The Silver Chair*, she encourages them to visit the giants of Harfang, describing them as kind and gentle.[18] Despite the mysterious and silent knight accompanying the queen, and despite Puddleglum's general distrust of strangers, the children are excited about visiting the giants for the Autumn Feast. And when they arrive, the giants do indeed seem gentle and dote upon the children. The king and queen are particularly pleased to receive the children. The trio of visitors is given food and drink, baths, and lodging.

The visit with the giants leads to another disturbing incident: The visitors discover they have been eating a talking stag, a realization that disturbs all of them but most of all Puddleglum because he is a native Narnian. The discovery that truly reveals the nature of the giants' deception, however, is made in the kitchen when Jill comes across a cookbook. To her horror, she finds the book open to "M" and skims the entry for "Man," described as a tasty dish eaten as part of the Autumn Feast.[19] Another entry tells how to cook marsh-wiggles. Fortunately, the two children and their friend are able to avoid being eaten by the giants, but their escape leads them to Underland, where they encounter a dishonest queen.

The queen of Underland. The ruler in Underland (a kingdom beneath Narnia) is really an evil witch who has killed King Caspian's wife and kidnapped Prince Rilian. Her goal, like that of the White Witch, Jadis, is to take control of Narnia. She attempts to do so by, among other things, acting dishonestly. She is deceptive in word and deed, using her powers of enchantment to blind Rilian to his true identity and enslave the Earthmen. She does not value truth and, therefore, does not value honesty. She is amoral. Her goal is to seek power by whatever means are necessary. In this way, too, she is like the White Witch and, in fact, is compared to Jadis by an owl.[20] One dwarf comments that witches like her have the same intentions, even though they may go about it differently.[21]

The queen of Underland's dishonest actions are many, such as the one described a few paragraphs back in which she convinces Puddleglum, Eustace, and Jill to visit the giants for the Autumn Feast. She also deceives Rilian and the Earthmen via her magic and, at times, takes the form of a green serpent.

Shift the ape. In *The Horse and His Boy*, Queen Lucy suggests letting the treacherous Prince Rabadash go free if he agrees to meet certain conditions, observing that he may turn out to be true to the agreement. King Edmund sarcastically replies that perhaps someday even apes will be true to their word.[22] It is possible that Lewis meant to foreshadow Shift the ape, who makes his appearance in *The Last Battle*. It may also be that Lewis was merely drawing from his extensive knowledge of literature. Lewis scholar Paul Ford observed, "The ape as a figure of great evil has at least one antecedent," and he went on to cite a sixteenth-century sermon in which the Antichrist is called an "ape."[23]

Whatever the case may be with the foreshadowing, Shift the ape is definitely dishonest. He tricks the donkey Puzzle into wearing a lion's skin in order to deceive the Narnians into thinking Aslan has come.[24] It has been so long since Aslan has appeared that the Narnians are uncertain of what to expect and go along with Shift's caricature of Aslan to a certain extent out of fear. Shift, however, plays an important role in the deception. Although at times he makes a number of slips of the tongue, forgetting to indicate that Aslan has ordered something and instead focusing on himself, he is quick to deceive with his words. As the ploy progresses, Shift attempts to pass himself off as a man and even wears clothing to bolster his deception.[25]

Perhaps Shift's greatest deception is his blending of the Calormene god Tash with Aslan. This comes in response to a question by a lamb: "What have we to do with the Calormenes? We belong to Aslan. They belong to Tash." The lamb, describing Tash as a beast with the head of a vulture and four arms who receives human sacrifices, wonders how Aslan and Tash could possibly have anything in common.[26] This sequence is reminiscent of 2 Corinthians 6:14-16:

> Do not be yoked together with unbelievers. For what do righteousness and wickedness have in common? Or what fellowship can light have with darkness? What harmony is there between Christ and Belial [Satan]? What does a believer have in common with an unbeliever? What agreement is there between the temple of God and idols?

Shift is not disturbed by the lamb's questions. After mocking and dismissing the lamb, the ape cleverly explains that Tash and Aslan are really the same.[27] Later the names are blended into "Tashlan" to further the ploy. This is a blasphemous deception, especially considering that Aslan is the creator of Narnia and the son of the Emperor-beyond-the-Sea. Of course, this is the effect Lewis is attempting to get across, as there are a number of references to Christian eschatology (beliefs about last things) that can be drawn from *The Last Battle.* These include the end of the world, the final judgment, and general apocalyptic elements, such as the presence of a false Aslan—an Antichrist not in a literal sense (the naive donkey Puzzle is duped) but as part of the overall deception involving Tashlan.

Shift's scheme is reminiscent of numerous warnings of Jesus concerning deception, such as "Many will come in my name, claiming, 'I am the Christ,' and will deceive many" and "Many false prophets will appear and deceive many people" (Matthew 24:5,11). Matthew 24:24 sums up the general situation in *The Last Battle*: "False Christs and false prophets will appear and perform great signs and miracles to deceive even the elect." The Narnians may be viewed as the "elect," yet many are deceived by Shift's lies.

The consequences of Shift's continuing vices, such as gluttony and dishonesty, are severe and result in his gradual loss of power to Rishda Tarkaan and Ginger the atheistic cat. In the end, miserable and confused, Shift is thrown into a mysterious barn, where he is devoured by the demon Tash.[28]

Good deceptions? There are some instances in the Chronicles of good characters turning to deception. Many, but not all, of these instances involve difficult situations during times of war or at least potential military peril.

In *The Horse and His Boy*, the Narnians are in Tashbaan and in a difficult situation. They are vastly outnumbered and fear that if Queen Susan rejects the marriage proposal of the volatile Calormene Prince Rabadash, the situation will rapidly deteriorate and lead to violence. So Tumnus the faun concocts a plan that involves preparations for a celebration aboard their ship, the *Splendour Hyaline*. By convincing the Calormenes that a party will be held aboard the ship, the Narnians are able to board their vessel without opposition. In short, they deceive the Calormenes in order to escape without shedding blood.[29]

In *The Last Battle*, Tirian, Eustace, and Jill disguise themselves as Calormenes in order to move more freely through areas of Narnia that have been occupied by enemy forces. The disguises help them blend in and assist them in rescuing Jewel the unicorn.[30]

In *The Horse and His Boy*, the main characters turn to using disguises as a means of escape. Initially, they are not in a military situation; however, they have good cause to flee (this is discussed in chapter 7). Their turning to deception via disguises in order to escape is not commented upon as being right or wrong.[31]

In all of these instances, the characters appear to be acting for the greater good. Furthermore, in no instance does Aslan directly sanction the use of dishonesty. He opposes it.[32]

Aslan and the God he represents desire honesty. We are not to be like Shift, the queen of Underland, and other dishonest characters in the Chronicles but rather are to be more like Lucy and Doctor Cornelius: truthful, honest, and full of integrity.

HONESTY INGRAINED

Although honesty will sometimes result in personal suffering, Christians are called to be honest. Doing the right thing in a fallen world does not guarantee freedom from unpleasant consequences. Consequently, when Lucy tells the truth about having been to Narnia, she sticks to it despite her siblings thinking that she is lying. Additionally, when the talking animals are celebrating over the feast provided by Father Christmas, they are honest regardless of the risk of being turned into stone. To them, the truth of what is happening—the coming of Father Christmas, the thawing of Narnia—is important, and they are unwilling to lie merely to appease the White Witch. In so doing, they make a difficult moral choice for the sake of truth. So, too, are Christians called to honesty despite unpleasant circumstances that may result.

Moreover, dishonesty has its consequences. Shift's deceptions lead him down a path of deterioration both physically and morally. In the end, his deceptions are his undoing. Deliberate dishonesty is a destroyer of personal character and relationships; it has no place in personal or social ethics.

When Tirian attempts to reveal the deceptive ploy of Shift, Rishda, and Ginger to a group of dwarfs, he is shocked by their skepticism and dismissal of Aslan. Tirian had no idea that the establishment of a fake Aslan would result in Narnians rejecting the true lion.[33] Likewise, we must be on guard lest we are deceived by "false Christs," "false prophets," "false doctrines," and false miracles (see Matthew 24:24; Mark 13:22; 1 Timothy 6:3). We must know what we believe and why. We must "examine everything carefully; hold fast to that which is good" (1 Thessalonians 5:21, NASB) because "the days are evil" (Ephesians 5:16) and "let no one in any way deceive" us (2 Thessalonians 2:3, NASB) with "fine-sounding arguments" (Colossians 2:4). We must be aware of the potential for self-deceit—for being dishonest with ourselves (see 1 Corinthians 3:18; James 1:22; 1 John 1:8). We are called to "pursue righteousness" (Isaiah 51:1; 1 Timothy 6:11; 2 Timothy 2:22), and such a pursuit includes the virtue of honesty.

When difficult ethical decisions arise regarding honesty and dishonesty, we have a number of options available to aid us in making a "right judgment" (John 7:24). For example, we should not neglect prayer and, at times, fasting to help us resolve ethical dilemmas. We may also consult with those we consider wise in such matters, such as a pastor or close friend. The Bible, while not addressing every possible situation we may encounter, may be consulted as well for ethical guidance.

In all of this, the development of character is paramount. By seeking to live virtuously, we are growing truth in our character. If we do this, when a difficult ethical situation arises, we are better prepared to cope with it based on the nurturing of our character that has already taken place. Lewis believed that every ethical action we make improves us or harms us and thus leads us closer to God and truth or further from Him. The wise choice is to "pursue righteousness."

But building a character of honesty takes more than sheer willpower; it also takes an understanding of the reality and significance of truth. Truth is real and it matters. As Douglas Groothuis observed, "Despite the truth-allergic pathologies of our postmodern culture, truth remains to be considered, known, and embraced."[34] Unfortunately, truth as absolute is too often dismissed or devalued. In its place we find moral relativism — the concept that there is no truth to guide our actions. Recapturing a sense of absolute truth rooted in God's nature is essential to honesty. God calls us to be truthful and considers truth important enough to include in the Ten Commandments (see Exodus 20:16).

In everyday life we will face situations that require a response on our part of either honesty or dishonesty. Sometimes we may have only seconds to make an ethical decision. That is why it is important to cultivate a character of virtue even in seemingly small matters. As we seek God's guidance and live accordingly, we will establish a pattern of virtuous living that, when the time comes, will move us in the direction of the right moral choice, even though it may not always be the easiest path. Of course, we will still stumble at times, but by God's grace, if we truly seek to live in a manner that is pleasing to Him, we will find that we are better prepared to make the right choice more often than not.

Reflection and Response Questions

1. Apart from Aslan, Lucy Pevensie is perhaps the most consistently honest character in the Chronicles. Which example of honesty in her life do you admire the most? Why? Do the people in your life think of you as an honest individual? Why or why not?

2. Is it ever acceptable to lie? If so, under what circumstances?

3. Have you been dishonest with others recently, either with words (lying) or by your actions (pretense)? What are the first steps you can take toward earning a reputation for truthfulness?

CHAPTER 5

MERCY *and* CRUELTY

Filled with maniacal passion, the White Witch sharpens her stone knife in preparation for the killing of the great lion. She revels in her victory. The fool, Aslan, has decided to die in the place of the traitorous Edmund. A crowd of wolves, ogres, wraiths, and other foul creatures surround the witch, anticipating the cruelty to come. The witch does not disappoint. Aslan, who offers no resistance, is rolled onto his side, his paws tied and his mouth muzzled. As he is being dragged to the Stone Table, the witch orders a further humiliation: The glorious mane of the beast is shaved. Hideous creatures hit, kick, and spit at the lion. At last, Aslan, creator of Narnia and son of the Emperor-beyond-the-Sea, is tied to the sacrificial table. The witch cannot resist one last torture, albeit a psychological one, prior to the sacrifice. She leans over Aslan and whispers that after she has killed him, she will kill Edmund anyway and reign over Narnia forever. Then her knife begins its work.[1]

In Narnian terms, the White Witch is the epitome of cruelty. She cares for only herself and the power to rule. With Aslan out of the way, she is eager to defeat Peter's army, the only thing (or so she thinks) that stands in the way of her victory. Just as she ruled in Charn as the Empress Jadis many years ago, so she desires to rule Narnia now. Ironically, in *The Magician's Nephew*, when Jadis is in a weakened state, she cries out for assistance, appealing for mercy.[2] She may not follow the Golden Rule, but when the situation suits her, she is certainly willing to appeal to an ethical standard.

If we were asked who epitomizes cruelty in our world, we might think of a historical figure such as Adolf Hitler or a contemporary one such as Osama bin Laden. Shocking acts of cruelty are the daily fare of news reporting. Yet we do not need to look outside ourselves for examples of cruelty; it exists in our own hearts. From taunting on the schoolyard to gossip among friends to power plays in the office, cruelty inflicts its harm in all our lives. We want to receive mercy and even (frequently) to give mercy, but all too often we are enmeshed in nets of cruelty exhibited between not only enemies but also friends.

C. S. Lewis was acquainted with both mercy and cruelty. Having fought in World War I, and having lived through the horrors of World War II, Lewis saw the best and the worst of people. Lewis, though, was a man of compassion. His stepson Douglas Gresham shared the story of how Lewis (whose nickname was Jack) and a friend were walking to a meeting one day when they were approached by a beggar. "The beggar asked them for some spare change whereupon Jack gave him everything he had. Once the beggar had gone, his friend said, 'You shouldn't have given that man all that money, Jack. He'll only spend it on drink.' Jack's reply—'Well, if I'd kept it, I would only have spent it on drink.'"

Remarking on the incident, Gresham noted Lewis's "enormous compassion and charity."[3]

Lewis clearly was a man of mercy, but he was also aware of the fallen human capacity to sin by various means, including acts of cruelty. As a result, the Chronicles often touch upon facets of mercy and cruelty. The insights gleaned from Lewis's writings on these topics provide lessons of lasting relevance.

HARD-HEARTED OR SOFT-HEARTED?

Before we look at mercy and cruelty as displayed in the Chronicles of Narnia, we need to consider what these qualities really mean. What do we mean by *mercy*? And what do we mean by *cruelty*?

Mercy can be defined as "displaying kindness beyond what is expected, with elements such as compassion, forgiveness, and leniency included." Though not always, mercy in some cases refers to the compassion shown to an enemy or offender. One dictionary defines mercy in part as "forbearance and compassion shown by one person to another who is in his power and who has no claim to receive kindness; kind and compassionate treatment in a case where severity is merited or expected" and as "God's pitiful forbearance towards his creatures and forgiveness of their offences."[4] Lewis understood the connection between mercy and forgiveness, particularly in viewing God's forgiveness as an act of mercy.[5] However, Lewis also associated mercy with justice (an aspect he brought out in the Chronicles) and pardon.[6]

Cruelty, on the other hand, is often defined as "being ready to inflict pain or expressing indifference to the suffering of others." Cruel individuals lack pity and deliberately cause suffering. One dictionary defines cruelty in part as "the quality of being cruel; disposition to inflict suffering; delight in or indifference to the pain or misery of others; mercilessness, hard-heartedness."[7] Cruelty may be physically or psychologically inflicted (the White Witch, for instance, employs both forms of cruelty).

Lewis offered many insights on cruelty. Cruelty is an aspect of the problem of evil, and when the behavior is exhibited between humans or even between a human and an animal, it is a problem of moral evil. Lewis recognized cruelty as another form of evil being parasitical on good. People are generally not cruel simply for the sake of being cruel. Instead, cruelty may be used as a means to accomplish an end, perhaps even an end that one might consider good. While a person may perform a good act simply because it is right, the same cannot be said for an act of cruelty or wickedness, which in its own way pursues good (or at least what one thinks is good) but in a manner that is wrong.[8] Good must first exist in order for evil to warp it, but evil cannot exist on its own in the same way that the original standard of good, rooted in God's nature, can exist.

MERCY AND CRUELTY IN BIBLICAL PERSPECTIVE

While gaining a better general understanding of the English word *mercy* is beneficial, it is also helpful to understand the term as used biblically. *The Dictionary of Biblical Imagery* provides a helpful definition of mercy as "aid rendered to someone who is miserable or needy, especially someone who is either in debt or without claim to favorable treatment."[9] Unfortunately, "in discussing the concept of mercy we face the common difficulty of such studies that there is more than one English word that expresses the idea (e.g., compassion, pity), that the one English word might be used to render a number of Greek and Hebrew roots, each with its own shade of meaning, and that the one Hebrew or Greek root might be translated by more than one word in English. In short, we have a number of overlapping concepts, between which it is not always easy to know where to draw the line."[10]

A distinction should be made between divine mercy and human mercy. The mercy of God is inexhaustible (see Lamentations 3:22, NRSV). Moreover, only God in His mercy is able to forgive the sins of the repentant.

In the Bible, God's mercy is displayed in numerous ways. His plan of redemption for fallen humanity, for instance, serves as an overarching biblical theme that has God's mercy as its basis. Jesus provided many examples of divine mercy, including His acts of healing, provision of food, ministry to outcasts, and so on. Jesus not only spoke of mercy but also took action and exhibited qualities of mercy. Jesus said,

> "Blessed are the merciful,
> for they will be shown mercy." (Matthew 5:7)

The parable of the Good Samaritan also provides an illustration of mercy (see Luke 10:25-37). Christ's most merciful act, however, was His sacrifice on the cross.

Human mercy is more limited in scope. Unlike the mercy of God, human mercy is exhaustible. Furthermore, as a consequence of our fallen nature, "a lack of mercy is more natural to the human condition."[11] As Blaise Pascal argued, human beings exhibit qualities of greatness and wretchedness—a paradox only Christianity adequately explains.[12] It is this element of greatness remaining in human beings that allows us to exhibit limited expressions of mercy.

Biblically, God is compassionate, merciful, and just. Job, however, in response to his many sufferings and obvious mental distress, referred to God as "cruel" when he said,

> You have become cruel to me;
> With the might of Your hand You persecute me.
> (Job 30:21, NASB)[13]

Additionally, in a prophecy referring to Babylon, Isaiah described the "day of the LORD" as "a cruel day, with wrath and fierce anger" (Isaiah 13:9). Although God is compassionate and merciful, He is also just and, because of this, demands judgment.

In the Bible, the term *cruel* is used many times of human beings (see Exodus 6:9; Psalm 71:4; Proverbs 27:4; Jeremiah 6:23). In discussing various words rendered as *wicked*, the *New Bible Dictionary* explains, "It denotes perversity of mind (Pr. 15:26; Rom. 1:29) by which the natural man surrenders himself to evil impulses (Ps. 10:1-11). Wickedness has its seat in the heart (Je. 17:9; Mk. 7:21-23), and is inspired by Satan (Mt. 13:19; 1 Jn. 3:12). It is progressive (Gen. 6:5) and contagious (1 Sa. 24:13) in its manifestation. The wicked man is utterly perverse, finding unholy delight in the infliction of injury (Pr. 21:10)."[14]

With this background of biblical understanding, we are

ready to look at examples of fictional mercy and cruelty in the Chronicles. The examples will show us what mercy and cruelty can look like in our own lives.

ASLAN'S HEART TOWARD OFFENDERS

Numerous examples of mercy are found in the Chronicles. Lucy, for example, often displays the virtue. In *The Lion, the Witch and the Wardrobe,* Lucy exhibits mercy following the battle with the army of the White Witch. In *The Horse and His Boy,* she displays mercy to Rabadash. And in *The Last Battle,* Lucy is merciful to the dwarfs.[15] However, because of the importance of divine mercy, this section will emphasize the kind of mercy represented by Aslan the lion.

Aslan and the fate of Edmund. Perhaps one of the clearest representations of divine mercy in the Chronicles (in certain ways paralleling the mercy of Christ's death) involves Aslan's sacrifice for Edmund. Although Christ's sacrifice was clearly on a grander scale, entailing more complex theological implications, in *The Lion, the Witch and the Wardrobe,* Lewis presents a similar incident.

Edmund has betrayed his brother and sisters and all of Narnia by allying with the White Witch. When Edmund is rescued, the witch demands the Deep Magic be satisfied in connection with the traitor.[16] When someone objects to her claims, she responds with anger and indicates that she has a right to satisfy the requirements of the Deep Magic by blood. Aslan acknowledges her just claim. In a private discussion, Aslan agrees to satisfy the requirements of the Deep Magic and later that evening is humiliated and then sacrificed by the witch.[17] This is when the witch is filled with maniacal passion and her knife goes about its work.

Despite Edmund's traitorous actions, Aslan exhibits mercy. This quality of mercy is a consistent aspect of his character.

Aslan and the fate of Prince Rabadash. In *The Horse and His Boy*, Prince Rabadash's unprovoked attack on Archenland fails. He is humiliated and captured but is treated well by King Lune of Anvard. The king realizes he must make a decision about the punishment of Rabadash. Someone recommends executing Rabadash by beheading, but King Edmund of Narnia, speaking from personal experience, points out that even traitorous people can change. Darrin, a lord of Archenland, takes a more calculated approach by suggesting that killing Rabadash could lead to war with the Tisroc. King Lune expresses his dislike for execution, and Lucy suggests he let Rabadash go so long as the prince promises to behave fairly in the future. The king agrees and asks for Rabadash to be brought before him. Hearing the offer, however, Rabadash responds poorly.[18] He calls them names and threatens them with violence.

At this point Aslan appears, warns the prince that continued outbursts will result in doom, and suggests that Rabadash receive the mercy of Lune and Edmund.[19] Aslan speaks the truth, knowing that justice must be done, but he offers Rabadash an opportunity to receive mercy. Unfortunately, though mercy can be offered, it is not always received. Rabadash responds angrily, calling Aslan a variety of names, including referring to him as a demon.[20] Aslan warns him again, but Rabadash continues with his tirade.

Here the transformation begins: Aslan turns Rabadash into a donkey, explaining, "Justice shall be mixed with mercy."[21] Rabadash must return to his home as a donkey and then, during a ceremony at the temple of his god Tash, will return to human form. However, if he travels more than ten miles from his home, Aslan informs him, he will once again turn into a donkey and will remain in that form permanently.[22]

Aslan and the fate of Narnia. In *The Last Battle*, Narnia comes to an end. Aslan stands at the opening of a door, and all the creatures of Narnia come to him and must stare at him. Lewis described this encounter as a series of creatures passing Aslan and essentially facing his judgment. Those who move to the lion's left, with expressions of anger and fear, enter darkness. Others enter a door on Aslan's right, gazing upon him with expressions of love.[23] This image is reminiscent of the New Testament description of judgment as a separation of the sheep from the goats: "He will put the sheep on his right and the goats on his left" (Matthew 25:33). The goats are deemed unworthy and "will go away to eternal punishment," while the sheep (or "righteous") will go "to eternal life" (verse 46).

The Last Battle depicts God's just judgment and mercy. Biblically speaking, "all have sinned and fall short of the glory of God" (Romans 3:23). It is only by God's grace and mercy through Jesus Christ and His sacrifice that anyone is allowed into the presence of the holy Lord. Aslan, like Christ, offers his grace and mercy to those willing to receive it, but it is not forced upon anyone (such as the dwarfs — see chapter 8).

"POISONOUS LITTLE BEASTS"

Along with Aslan and other merciful characters, such as Lucy, Narnia is filled with characters more cruel than merciful, at least at times. From these characters, we learn by negative example what can become of us if we choose cruelty over Christlike mercy.

The White Witch. Jadis, the White Witch, is cruel in thought, word, and deed. Her cruelty includes cruelty to the divine, humans, Talking Beasts and other citizens of Narnia, "dumb" beasts, and even entire civilizations. Moreover, she is cruel to her enemies as well as to her minions. It can even be said that she is cruel to the environment in seeking to control it by making it always winter for a hundred years.

The witch's cruelty directed toward Aslan is of particular interest because of his association with Christ. Though it is not clear how much the witch knows about Aslan, *The Magician's Nephew* explains that she witnessed Aslan create Narnia. In fact, upon first meeting Aslan during his creation of Narnia, Jadis throws an iron bar at him with the intention of stopping him.[24] She relishes the opportunity to mock and kill Aslan upon the Stone Table, as described at the beginning of this chapter.

The White Witch appears to have a particular hatred for humans.[25] In *The Lion, the Witch and the Wardrobe*, she fears an ancient prophecy foretelling the arrival of four humans who will cause her downfall. When her plan to capture and kill the four Pevensie children is thwarted, she decides that killing one captive (Edmund) will be enough to stop fulfillment of the prophecy. This involves an attempt at human sacrifice using a ceremonial knife.[26] Her cruelty to humans is displayed in other ways as well. She calls Edmund names and later strikes him.[27] In *The Magician's Nephew*, Jadis grabs Aunt Letty (Andrew's sister) and throws her.[28]

Instances of the witch's cruelty against the citizens of Narnia are many. Perhaps the most memorable example is found in *The Lion, the Witch and the Wardrobe*. When she comes across a group of talking Narnian animals feasting and learns that they were visited by Father Christmas, she is enraged and turns the creatures into stone.[29] As evidenced by the many statues in and around her home, she has turned many others to stone also.[30] In another instance of her cruelty to the citizens of Narnia, the witch sends Maugrim (a wolf and the captain of the witch's secret police) to the home of the beavers, instructing him to kill any he finds in the home.[31]

While the issue of cruelty to animals is addressed in more detail later, it is important to note the cruel manner in which the witch treats animals. After Jadis is brought to England, she commandeers a hansom cab and flogs a horse mercilessly.[32] In *The Lion, the Witch and the Wardrobe*, the witch displays cruelty to her two reindeer via her dwarf servant.[33]

Jadis also exhibits cruelty on a global, genocidal scale. When Digory and Polly travel to the world of Charn and, as a result of Digory's actions, Jadis is awakened, we learn more about the fall of the world. Jadis speaks of dungeons and torture chambers and tells the children the story of a banquet hall and how her great-grandfather killed seven hundred nobles because of their potential for rebellion.[34] Later, speaking again of Charn, she mentions slaves being whipped and the sound of drums used in sacrificial ceremonies.[35] She then speaks of a terrible battle between her armies and those of her sister (discussed in chapter 6).

Jadis expresses no remorse over the sufferings of Charn and its people.[36] In fact, she views her subjects as hers to do with as she pleases, placing herself above norms of right and wrong because of her status as queen. While she admits it might be wrong for ordinary individuals to do certain things, such is not the case for her.[37] This parallels a similar scene with Uncle Andrew, wherein he excuses himself from rules and observes that in some instances, ethical rules that apply to others don't apply to sophisticated people such as himself.[38]

Edmund. In the characters of Edmund Pevensie and Eustace Scrubb, Lewis presented qualities of human cruelty. Granted, the cruelty exhibited by the children is not of the same severity as that of the White Witch. Nevertheless, they serve as examples of not only human cruelty but also redemption (see chapter 8).

In *The Lion, the Witch and the Wardrobe*, after Lucy tells of entering Narnia through the wardrobe, her siblings do not believe her. At this point, we are told of Edmund's spite, as demonstrated by his cruel teasing of Lucy.[39] Later, Peter confirms Edmund's spite and past cruelty, thus establishing a pattern of cruel behavior in Edmund.[40] Perhaps one of the cruelest actions taken by Edmund — described as one of the worst actions in the story — occurs after he enters the wardrobe and finds himself in Narnia.[41] He meets with the White Witch, has his fill of Turkish Delight (a gelatin-like candy), and allies himself with the queen. He meets Lucy in Narnia prior to their return to their own world. She is naturally excited to have someone to corroborate her story, but in a surprisingly cruel move, Edmund does no such thing. Instead, he tells Peter and Susan that he has merely been playing along with Lucy — their experience was not real.[42] Lucy is devastated by this act of betrayal and emotional cruelty.

Not long after, when all four children find their way into

Narnia through the wardrobe, it is discovered that Edmund had indeed been to Narnia before. When Peter makes the comment, "Of all the poisonous little beasts," Edmund becomes determined to seek revenge.[43] When the children are meeting with Mr. and Mrs. Beaver, Edmund slips away to visit the White Witch. Of this incident, Paul Ford wrote, "He leaves to accomplish his betrayal of his brother and sisters into the witch's hands before he hears the explanation of who she is. Lewis is careful to distinguish Edmund's motives at this point: he doesn't want any real harm to come to them but (besides power and pleasure) he does want revenge on Peter, and for the witch to prefer him to the others. But 'deep down inside' he really knows how cruel and evil she is."[44] Despite this internal knowledge, Edmund presses forward with his plan. Mercy is nowhere to be found in him, though that will change.

Eustace. In the character of Eustace Clarence Scrubb, we see what Edmund may have been like prior to his transformation in Narnia. We are told in *The Voyage of the "Dawn Treader"* that Eustace has no friends, has been raised in a nontraditional manner (for example, he calls his parents by their first names), and attends a dysfunctional school called Experiment House. Eustace is fond of animals so long as they are not alive. We are also told that although he has no particular love for his cousins, he was pleased that they were visiting, because he enjoyed bullying them.[45]

In one instance of cruelty and meanness, Eustace enjoys an opportunity to tease Edmund and Lucy about Narnia. He comes up with a limerick to mock them. When he asks Lucy if she likes a picture and she says that she does, Eustace expresses his hatred of it.[46] After Eustace is transported to Narnia — or, more specifically, to the Narnian ship *Dawn Treader* — he makes a nuisance of himself, complaining a great deal and displaying a lack of appreciation for the mercy shown him, such as Lucy bringing him something to ease his seasickness.[47]

While on the ship, Eustace performs another act of cruelty. This time his target is the talking Narnian mouse Reepicheep. While Reepicheep is sitting down, Eustace comes up with the idea of grabbing the tail of Reepicheep and swinging him around. Eustace carries out his plan, but it does not go exactly as expected. After being punished by Reepicheep (the talking mouse repeatedly hits Eustace with a sword), Eustace runs away and, despite the cruelty on his part that angered Reepicheep, claims he has a right to demand that Reepicheep be punished or killed.[48] Thankfully, Eustace is a reformed character in *The Silver Chair* and *The Last Battle*.

Uncle Andrew and cruelty to animals. In *The Magician's Nephew*, Andrew (Digory's uncle) is obsessed with seeking power, manipulating the world of the occult for his purposes, and living his life by the philosophy that the ends justify the means. His cruelty to animals in all of this is plain. While he is explaining how he had to test magic dust contained in a box allegedly from Atlantis, he recounts his use of guinea pigs in experimentation, observing that some died, while others blew up in small explosions. Digory responds by proclaiming that such actions are cruel.[49] Andrew chides Digory for missing the point and adds that the guinea pigs served their purpose. He implies that because he owned them, he could do what he liked with them, much like Jadis with her human subjects in Charn. In Andrew's mind, the ethical implication of using guinea pigs for experimentation purposes is a nonissue. He is not so much overtly cruel as indifferent and oblivious to his cruelty.

The experimentation with guinea pigs is not the only example of Andrew's cruelty to animals. Later in the book, after witnessing Aslan's creation of Narnia, Andrew considers what he might do to harm Aslan, intimating the use of a firearm. He also admires Jadis for throwing an iron bar at Aslan, but he is rebuked by Polly.[50]

Lewis pondered the question of causing pain to animals in several works in addition to the Chronicles. In an essay on vivisection, Lewis explained that efforts to justify cruelty to animals place humans on the same level as beasts.[51] He wrote a reply to criticisms of his position on animal pain by C. E. M. Joad, a philosopher at the University of London.[52] Lewis also raised the matter of vivisection and animal cruelty in *That Hideous Strength*, where he observed that the fictional organization N.I.C.E. (the National Institute for Coordinated Experiments) was involved in vivisection on an extensive scale.[53]

Some of Lewis's most cogent insights on the topic appear in *The Problem of Pain*. In this work, he summarized three issues that humans are presented with in relation to evil and suffering of animals. First, there is the matter of determining what kind of suffering that animals experience. Second, there is the question of how such suffering begins to affect animals in the first place. Third, there is the issue of how the suffering of animals relates to God's justice.[54] Later in the book, he noted that although human beings are charged with "dominion" over animals (Genesis 1:26,28), we are still capable of warping our dominion by abusing creatures.[55]

Cruelty indeed represents a warping of the human nature God intended for us. Through the power of God's Spirit, though, we can be made over into ones who exhibit mercy to others as Christ exhibited mercy to us.

FOLLOWING CHRIST IN MERCY

In the Chronicles, as in his other writings, Lewis argued for and assumed the truth of natural law. When Edmund attempts to manufacture excuses to explain the betrayal of his siblings, we are told that "deep down inside him he really knew that the White Witch was bad and cruel."[56] Edmund demonstrates in part what Paul explained in Romans, namely that every human being, created as we are in the image of God, inherently knows that God exists, that He has established moral law, and that we break this law (see Romans 1:19-21; 2:14-15). Because of this fact, "deep down inside" Edmund possesses enough knowledge to know the true nature of the witch, despite her attempts to convince him otherwise, as well as the inherent wrongness of his betrayal. We, too, know on some level deep inside when something is right or something is wrong.

Of course, Lewis knew this line of argumentation could serve only as a step on the path to Christianity. He said as much in *Mere Christianity* when he noted that he was still a long way from proving the God of the Bible.[57] Nevertheless, it is an important point and a stepping-stone for many skeptics in search of truth. It creates, as Dallas Willard has said in arguing for God, an "ontologically haunted universe. It is haunted by unnerving possibilities."[58] Something is out there, and it just might be God.

Lewis's examples of mercy in the Chronicles serve as

reminders of the answer to the question that sparked the parable of the Good Samaritan: Who is our neighbor? As Jesus illustrated, everyone is our neighbor, deserving of our mercy and compassion (see Luke 10:29-37). Furthermore, Aslan's mercy reminds us of God's mercy, demonstrated most clearly in the person of Christ. In striving to imitate His example, we must show mercy and compassion through our prayers as well as our actions.

The Chronicles teach us that even though there are degrees of cruelty (such as the extreme cruelty of the White Witch contrasted with the lesser cruelties of Uncle Andrew, Eustace, and Edmund), all cruelty is wrong in the eyes of God and in light of His moral law. Christians have a duty to not only avoid acts of cruelty but also attempt to put an end to cruelty wherever it may be found. And if the world disagrees with us, we are to "obey God rather than any human authority" (Acts 5:29, NRSV).

At the end of the parable of the Good Samaritan, Christ asked, "Which of these three do you think was a neighbor to the man who fell into the hands of robbers?" The "expert in the law" answered, "The one who had mercy on him." Jesus' response is telling: "Go and do likewise" (Luke 10:36-37). To alleviate suffering by acts of mercy and compassion is something everyone is called to do.

It is all very well to speak of the importance of mercy, but how does one "go and do likewise" when it comes to this virtue? It is not an exaggeration to say that love is the foundation of Christian ethics. Where there is love, there is mercy. When Jesus was asked, "Of all the commandments, which is the most important?" He replied, "The most important one . . . is this: 'Hear, O Israel, the Lord our God, the Lord is one. Love the Lord your God with all your heart and with all your soul and with all your mind and with all your strength.' The second is this: 'Love your neighbor as yourself.' There is no commandment greater than these" (Mark 12:28-31). In the same vein, Paul wrote, "If I speak in the tongues of men and of angels, but have not love, I am only a resounding gong or a clanging cymbal" (1 Corinthians 13:1). So it goes with love and mercy.

Love is the core of virtue. Because we love God, we love His standards of virtue and, in turn, will love others. But this love must flow from our relationship with the Lord. We must first seek Him and His righteousness in order for His love to work in our lives. As Jesus noted in the passage quoted above, every fiber of our being must seek to love God, for only then will we properly love others as ourselves. The key to mercy is love.

Reflection and Response Questions

1. In what ways does Aslan's mercy toward others in the Narnia stories remind you of Christ's mercy toward you? Has Christ's mercy inspired you to show mercy toward others? Identify at least one specific time when you have shown mercy to someone in the last month.

2. Read the story of the Good Samaritan in Luke 10:25-37. Afterward, spend time in prayer, asking God to show you what it will mean for you to "go and do likewise," as verse 37 says to do.

Chapter 6

Peace *and* War

In *The Magician's Nephew*, Digory Kirke and Polly Plummer stare at a dry hollow in the ground where a magical pool once led to another world. Aslan explains that the pool has disappeared because the world is no more. He then offers a warning to Digory and Polly about their own world, our earth: It, too, could one day be gone, perhaps as a result of our own actions.[1]

This is how that other world—the one represented by the vanished pool—came to its end: Queen Jadis ruled over Charn, the greatest city in that world, but war broke out between Jadis and her sister. Despite an agreement by both women that magic would not be used in the war, Jadis's sister chose to use it. At first, Jadis fought by means other than magic, including the callous and ruthless sacrifice of her armies. The final battle lasted for days in Charn. Finally, with her armies defeated, Jadis resorted to the powerful, dark magic of the Deplorable Word. She uttered that word, and every living thing in the world was destroyed except for Jadis herself.[2]

As Digory and Polly stare at the hollow in the ground, Polly suggests to Aslan that the people of earth aren't as bad off, morally speaking, as those in the world destroyed by Jadis. His response is sobering: Perhaps the people of earth are not at the same point of destructive behavior as the people of Charn were, but they are moving in that direction. Aslan even suggests to these Victorian-era children that one day, humans might discover something as bad as the Deplorable Word and use it as Jadis did.[3]

Although a World War I veteran and well aware of the horrors of war, C. S. Lewis did not think the atomic bomb — perhaps our "Deplorable Word" — introduced any particularly new or unique circumstances. He was concerned, though, that some people were overly worried about the potential for nuclear war and were allowing the thought of it to poison the joys of life. Because we are all going to die anyway, there is no point in fretting.[4] Lewis believed we should not huddle in fear over the potential for nuclear war but instead go about our business, living our lives sensibly and as best we can.[5]

War and peace continue to alternate in human history in our day, even though warfare may have taken on new forms, such as war on terrorism. As we look at the ways war and peace are handled by the characters in the Chronicles of Narnia, we discover much about how we can live well as Christians regardless of what is happening in the political sphere. We seek peace at all times and accept war when we must.

JUST WAR, RIGHTEOUS PEACE

Because of the times he lived through — encompassing both world wars — Lewis often wrote of peace in relation to war. But his writings also indicate a keen understanding of peace in other senses, such as peace with God. In *Mere Christianity*, he wrote that human beings are designed to run on God and, consequently, we cannot truly be at peace unless our peace comes from Him.[6] Lewis also greatly valued the power of prayer. It is clear that he found strength as well as peace in times of solitude and prayer. In relation to war, however, Lewis found the evidence weighing against pacifism.[7] Lewis not only voluntarily participated in World War I but also believed it was his duty to support World War II, which he believed to be a just war.

Although Lewis supported war under certain conditions, he was by no means unfamiliar with its negative consequences. Memories of his military service in World War I, for instance, haunted his dreams.[8] But Lewis believed that despite war life must go on and that war does not really create a new situation for human beings, though it does often bring home the reality of death (not necessarily a negative result).[9] In *The Screwtape Letters*, the devil Screwtape suggests that war is not necessarily a beneficial situation from the perspective of devils because war reminds people of their mortality, while in times of peace they may be diverted from such important thoughts and instead be drawn to worldliness.[10]

Lewis believed that "if war is ever lawful, then peace is sometimes sinful."[11] He thus appears to have accepted the just-war theory, a traditional Christian approach to war and peace. The just-war theory cannot be found in any one place in the Bible, but its supporters would argue that all of its elements can be substantiated from principles of Scripture.

A TIME FOR WAR AND A TIME FOR PEACE

In a prophetic passage in the Old Testament, we read that the Messiah would be called the "Prince of Peace" (Isaiah 9:6). But in the New Testament, the Messiah is depicted as a warrior on a white horse, symbolically described as having a sword in his mouth "with which to strike down the nations" (Revelation 19:15). Which view of Christ is correct? Is He the Prince of Peace, or is He a warrior who wields a sword of judgment? Fortunately, there are other options than simply choosing between the two portrayals. Christ is the Prince of Peace, but He is also just and, consequently, administers justice when necessary.

That the Bible uses warlike imagery to depict divine justice is clear, but what does the Bible have to say about peace and war? The Bible contains a number of accounts of warfare.[12] In many of these instances, God called the Israelites to war on His behalf. Sometimes God is depicted as a divine warrior who uses His power to thwart evil (see Exodus 15:3). In Old Testament times, "Israel and the entire ancient Near East knew almost constant warfare. Armies were always on the move, either in the interest of expanding imperial territories or defending against foreign encroachment."[13]

An analysis of such encounters reveals various kinds of warfare on the part of Israel. As Scott Rae observed, "Some of these wars were designed to secure Israel's boundaries and could be called preventive strikes (2 Sam. 5:17-25; 11:1-2). Others were clearly wars of national defense, fending off the attacks of a belligerent foreign nation (1 Kings 20). But others were aggressive in nature, designed to push Israel's enemies out of the Promised Land (Josh. 6–12)."[14]

The New Testament, while at times including images of warfare, often speaks of peace.[15] In the Sermon on the Mount, Christ said, "Blessed are the peacemakers" (Matthew 5:9), while in Mark 9:50, He said, "Be at peace with each other." In John 14:27, Jesus told His disciples, "Peace I leave with you; my peace I give you." And in a passage familiar even to many non-Christians, Jesus said, "I tell you, Do not resist an evil person. If someone strikes you on the right cheek, turn to him the other also" (Matthew 5:39). Christian pacifists will often cite such passages in defense of their position. Those with opposing views, such as Lewis, generally take the position that such verses are in reference to personal peace, such as getting along with neighbors, and are not directly relevant to warfare on a national scale.

Over the course of church history, some Christians have held to pacifism, while others have advocated warfare if specific conditions are met. While just-war theory from a distinctly Christian perspective began with Augustine, it developed more systematically over the years (particularly in the Middle Ages). The classic position is generally identified by seven points: "A war is generally considered just if and only if it is waged for a just cause, is motivated by a just intention, comes as the last resort, is pursued by a legitimate governmental authority, has limited ends in view, exempts noncombatants from attack and carries a reasonable hope of success."[16]

In an age of potential nuclear warfare, the implementation and interpretation of some of these points is difficult. For instance, with a weapon as powerful as a nuclear bomb, it is difficult, if not impossible, to guarantee the safety of noncombatants.

Nevertheless, for Christians who reject pacifism, just-war theory and its contemporary variations are often helpful in determining a balanced course of action in the face of continuing strife.

Ecclesiastes 3:8 notes there is "a time for war and a time for peace." Although the ideal state of affairs is peace, Christians supporting the just-war theory counter that in a fallen world, there are times when war is necessary to defeat greater evil. If this is true, then, as Lewis points out, there are times when peace may be sinful.

Part of the good news of the Christian worldview, though, is that evil will ultimately be defeated by God.

> Nation will not take up sword against nation,
> nor will they train for war anymore.
> (Isaiah 2:4; Micah 4:3)

At the end of *The Last Battle*, Lewis painted a wonderful picture of such a day when he described the joy of being in Aslan's country.

Narnia is helpful to us in many ways in the manner in which it reflects our experiences with war and with peace.

PEACEMAKERS IN THE CHRONICLES

Readers of the Chronicles of Narnia may get the impression that strife and warfare are regular occurrences in Narnia. This, in fact, is what Jill Pole thinks in *The Last Battle.* Whenever English children are called into Narnia, there always seems to be a crisis that inevitably involves some kind of strife. But as Jewel the unicorn observes, throughout Narnia's history, there has been much peace and stability. It is only every now and then that serious trouble arises. As Jewel explains it, during the times when the aid of the children was not needed, Narnia experienced prolonged periods of peace when nothing much eventful occurred.[17] There were centuries of happy times involving dancing, feasting, and tournaments.[18]

The Golden Age of Narnia. Peace is clearly valued by Narnians. The Golden Age of Narnia (a term used to describe the period when Narnia was ruled by Peter, Susan, Edmund, and Lucy) is referred to fondly several times in the Chronicles.[19] The Golden Age is a time of peace following the Hundred Years of Winter, when Narnia was ruled by the White Witch. It is a time when the kings and queens rule justly and peace reigns.[20] The Golden Age is also an age of freedom when citizens are allowed to live freely—within the parameters of good laws, no doubt. It is also during the Golden Age that incursions of giants into Narnian territory are driven back, indicating that even in an age of peace, vigilance must be kept and hostile intruders repelled. Another significant aspect of the Golden Age involves cultivating peaceful relations with other countries.[21] A potential downside of such a time of peace is that by the time of *The Horse and His Boy*, which takes place during the Golden Age, some Narnians have become complacent about potential attacks from hostile neighboring countries, such as the empire of Calormen.[22]

Aslan and peace. The culmination of the Chronicles is the peace and joy of entering Aslan's country, which corresponds to the Christian concept of "a new heaven and a new earth" (Revelation

21:1). Our world will end, but when it does, God's plans will come to fruition: Evil will be done away with, and there will be peace and joy for those who believed in Christ and accepted His offer of salvation. The prospect ahead of Aslan's followers in *The Last Battle* is of just such peace and joy. As on earth, however, Narnia's worldly existence (which in Lewis's Neoplatonic sense is a shadow of the reality to come) must address times of strife.

While Aslan is no warmonger, neither is he a pacifist. He sanctions warfare to overcome or deter evil. Like Christ, Aslan has the capacity for peace and the capacity for war. Consequently, Aslan has beautiful and large velvetlike paws, but he can also reveal his fierce claws when needed, such as when he enters battle in *The Lion, the Witch and the Wardrobe* and kills the White Witch.[23] Likewise, his powerful jaws have the capacity to crush but can also be used playfully, as when Aslan picks up the dwarf Trumpkin in *Prince Caspian*.[24] Aslan desires peace but knows that ultimate peace will not come until Narnia draws to a close and his followers enter the real Narnia in his own country, where there is no war. As Reepicheep is preparing to enter Aslan's country, he seems to understand this concept, as he willingly leaves behind his sword—an uncharacteristic act for such a courageous mouse.[25]

JUST AND UNJUST WARS IN NARNIA

Wars and battles occur throughout the Chronicles, not only providing an element of adventure and tension but also offering glimpses into Lewis's overall philosophy of warfare. Both just and unjust wars and military actions are present in the books. An example of unjust violence is Prince Rabadash's unprovoked attack upon Anvard. Another example of an unjust war involves the invasion of Narnia, with the intent to conquer, by the Calormen Empire in *The Last Battle* (this incident also takes place during a time of peace between the countries and involves a covert invasion).

Aslan is not opposed to a just war and, at times, even offers military advice. It is, however, in his character to oppose military atrocities. An example of just wars includes King Peter's battles against hostile giants, described peripherally in *The Lion, the Witch and the Wardrobe* and *The Horse and His Boy* — a situation that is again faced during the rule of King Caspian.[26]

As for the violence resulting from warfare as depicted in the Chronicles, Lewis believed that such horrors should not be hidden from children. Instead, children should know about the reality of warfare and its consequences.

Lewis further revealed his support of just warfare by choosing to have Father Christmas provide gifts of armament to the children: Peter receives a sword and shield; Susan receives a bow and arrows and a magic horn; Lucy receives a dagger and a cordial filled with a powerful healing potion. Father Christmas stresses that these are not playthings, and Peter solemnly receives his gifts.[27]

Aslan and war. The Christ figure, Aslan, actively supports and participates in war. In *The Lion, the Witch and the Wardrobe*, for instance, Aslan gives Peter advice on how best to prepare for the coming battle with the White Witch.[28] Aslan also approves of Peter's use of violence against the wolf who attacks Susan, and he knights Peter after the boy kills the wolf.[29] After Aslan is resurrected, he breathes upon the statues in the witch's home, thus reviving them with the purpose of not only rescuing them but also recruiting them as an army to battle the witch.[30] Finally, Aslan actively participates in the battle, pouncing upon the witch and killing her.[31]

But the war against the witch is not the only time when Aslan engages in battle. In *Prince Caspian*, Aslan once again shows support for just warfare during the War of Deliverance. A scene in *The Silver Chair* offers further evidence of Aslan's support of warfare. After the queen of Underland is slain by Prince Rilian, Puddleglum, and Eustace, Rilian refuses to wear the enchanted armor even though he may face battle. He does, however, consider it wise to take his sword and shield. Upon retrieving his shield, he notices that it has been transformed from black to silver and that a symbol has appeared on the shield: the red lion, representative of Aslan.[32] In *The Last Battle*, Aslan is not actively on the scene in Narnia as he is in the other books. Nevertheless, his support of just warfare is clear from the previous examples as well as throughout the Chronicles.

The war against the White Witch. At the time of *The Lion, the Witch and the Wardrobe*, the White Witch—a merciless tyrant who regularly turns talking beasts and other Narnians into stone—has reigned over Narnia for a hundred years. Servants of the witch make an unprovoked attack against Aslan's forces, and after the witch has killed Aslan, she does not hesitate to attack Peter's army with the intent of eradicating all opposition.

The war against the White Witch is just. The cause and intention are just: the removal of a tyrant, and freedom for the oppressed. The war is a last resort, because for a hundred years the witch has oppressed the Narnians and they now find themselves in a situation in which she will lead her armies against them with the intent of destroying them. The war is approved by Aslan, who represents divine authority, as well as by Peter, who represents governmental authority. And the war is limited in scope, intended to stop the forces of evil from ruling Narnia and oppressing the citizens.[33]

The War of Deliverance. The central plot of *Prince Caspian* involves what is referred to in *The Last Battle* as the War of Deliverance.[34] King Miraz, uncle to Caspian, rules Narnia as a result of treachery and the murder of Caspian's father. When Prunaprismia, wife of Miraz, gives birth to a son, we learn that Miraz plans to murder Caspian, who is the rightful heir to the throne. Caspian flees to the woods, where he encounters for the first time talking beasts and other creatures he has heard of only in stories.

The War of Deliverance is a civil war, described as a rebellion by Trumpkin the dwarf.[35] Upon learning that Caspian, true heir to the throne, has come to the woods as an enemy of Miraz, the talking beasts and other creatures rally to his side but are hopelessly outnumbered by King Miraz and his Telmarine army. Caspian uses the magic horn of Susan to summon help. Peter, Susan, Edmund, and Lucy return to Narnia. In an effort to minimize bloodshed and defeat Miraz and his army despite Caspian's being outnumbered, Peter develops a plan to challenge Miraz to single combat in order to decide the victor of the war.[36] Because of his pride, Miraz accepts and is defeated (though in the end he is killed by one of his own men, not Peter).

Aslan does not participate directly in the final battle of the War of Deliverance (known as the second Battle of Beruna) by way of combat as he did in *The Lion, the Witch and the Wardrobe*, but he clearly supports Caspian's side. For instance, he guides Lucy and the others in the right direction so they may meet up with Caspian. Also, by bringing Bacchus and asking him to destroy a bridge that is imprisoning a river god, he effectively cuts off an attempted escape of the remaining Telmarine army. Aslan's mere appearance on the battlefield frightens the Telmarines terribly. The lion indicates his support of Caspian and, with the Telmarines defeated, officially appoints him king of Narnia.[37]

Unlike the survivors of the evil army in *The Lion, the Witch and the Wardrobe*, who are hunted down after the battle because of their continued hostility, the Telmarines in *Prince Caspian* are given the option of staying in Narnia so long as they acknowledge the rule of Caspian (and possession of the land by the talking beasts and other Narnian creatures) or returning to their own world via a door made by Aslan.[38]

War and the queen of Underland. One example of an unjust war (or attempt at war) is the planned war of the queen of Underland in *The Silver Chair*. She concocts an involved plan to overthrow Narnia and rule it presumably in much the same way as the White Witch did. She begins by killing the queen of Narnia (Ramandu's daughter) and then casting a spell upon the queen's son, Prince Rilian, and kidnapping him. For several years, the queen prepares her rise to power, which involves magically enslaving the creatures of Underland to serve as her army and workforce to dig a tunnel that will emerge beneath Narnia in order for the army to launch a surprise attack. The queen then plans to rule with the enchanted Rilian, the rightful heir to the throne of Narnia, at her side.

As in the War of Deliverance, Aslan is clearly on the side of the Narnians, as shown by his calling of Eustace and Jill, accompanied by the marsh-wiggle Puddleglum, to come to the aid of Rilian. As previously mentioned, Aslan's support is underscored when Rilian's black shield magically turns silver and the red symbol of a lion appears on it.

The Battle of Anvard. In *The Horse and His Boy*, Lewis presents another example of an unjust war. This time, an unjustified attack is planned by Prince Rabadash, eldest son of the Tisroc of Calormen, on the neighboring kingdom of Archenland during a time of peace. Specifically, Rabadash plans to attack the castle Anvard with his army of two hundred men on horseback, thereby taking control of Archenland and establishing a foothold to attack and conquer Narnia at a future date. The immediate plan involves taking Anvard and then marching on to Narnia to kidnap Queen Susan so that Rabadash can marry her against her will. Neither attack — on Archenland or on Narnia — is justified.

What makes Rabadash's plan to attack Anvard particularly disturbing is the ruthless manner in which he plans to carry it out. While Rabadash intends to kill as few as possible upon reaching Narnia (only because of his father's orders and the greater plot to conquer Narnia at a future time), he instructs his men to kill every male in Anvard, even children and infants.[39] Aslan again favors the Narnians by guiding Shasta in time to warn Anvard of the attack and also to alert talking beasts and, eventually, King Edmund of the surprise attack. As a result, Anvard is prepared,

Edmund arrives with an army, and Rabadash is defeated.

Aggressive, violent behavior like that of Rabadash is just as common in our world as in Narnia. Stories of Narnian wars remind us of the importance of pursuing peace and justice on earth.

Blessed Are the Peacemakers

Regardless of one's position on pacifism and the just-war theory, Christians are called to be peacemakers (see Matthew 5:9). As such, we should cultivate a character of peace. While war allows opportunity for evil, it also allows opportunity for development of moral character by such virtues as courage. Even the vice of cowardice in warfare may eventually lead to repentance.

Christ said there would be "wars and rumors of wars" (Matthew 24:6; Mark 13:7) but that such events should not alarm us. The peace of the Christian lies in trusting in Christ and the peace He provides: "Peace I leave with you; my peace I give you. I do not give to you as the world gives. Do not let your hearts be troubled and do not be afraid" (John 14:27). Even at times of darkness and despair, we must trust in God as Prince Rilian trusted in Aslan in *The Silver Chair*, knowing that Aslan would be with Rilian and his allies even if the lion meant them to die.[40]

Like Aslan, God is multifaceted. Aslan's velvetlike paws and powerful jaws can be used for expressing love, but the claws can come out as needed and his jaws can crush injustice. Likewise, God is a God of love (see 1 John 4:8) as well as a God of justice (see Psalm 45:6).

Furthermore, war is not limited to the physical realm. Revelation 12:7 mentions "war in heaven" and goes on to describe a struggle between "Michael and his angels" against "the dragon and his angels." Additionally, passages such as Ephesians 6:10-18 highlight the reality of spiritual warfare: "For our struggle is not against flesh and blood, but against the rulers, against the authorities, against the powers of this dark world and against the spiritual forces of evil in the heavenly realms" (Ephesians 6:12). Christians must be prepared to wage war in this unseen battle through prayer and dedication to God's revealed truth.

While most of us are not in a position to impact decisions about warfare at a national level (other than through basic citizen activism, such as participating in elections), we can do something about cultivating a character of peace in our lives. Two aspects of C. S. Lewis's spiritual life are helpful in this regard.

A devout man, Lewis spent on average as much as an hour per day in prayer. Spending regular time in prayer, alone and with others, is one way to cultivate a character of peace. But we must go beyond superficial prayers offered hastily perhaps before meals or before going to bed.[41] We must learn and put into practice sound approaches to prayer. We can begin by setting aside time each day for prayer.

Lewis also spent a good deal of time studying God's Word, which offers yet another method of cultivating peace. For instance, the Psalms (which Lewis wrote about in his book *Reflections on the Psalms*)[42] contain many references to peace. One of these references is Psalm 34:14, which tells us,

> Turn from evil and do good;
> seek peace and pursue it.

Consistently reading the Bible, and then reflecting on its truths, fills us with light and dispels the darkness. It restrains our traits that result in strife.

In a world filled with distractions and diversions, we can also make a concerted effort to cultivate opportunities for peace in our lives. We may, for instance, curb the amount of time spent watching television or listening to music, in order to set aside times of silence that will allow for peaceful, holy reflection. The world around us often assaults our senses with noises, images, and a myriad of opportunities for diversion that do little to cultivate a character of peace. We are conditioned to crave entertainment and amusements. Approached from a balanced perspective, such things are not bad per se, but often then there is no place for peace in our fast-paced schedules.

Unless we make efforts to cultivate peace in our character, more often than not what little peace we may possess will be drowned out by a cacophonous world.[43]

Reflection and Response Questions

1. What is your reaction to the stories of battles and fighting in the Chronicles? Do you find them exciting and enjoyable, or

do they make you uncomfortable? Why is that? Identify an insight that the stories of peace and warfare in the Chronicles give you about peace and warfare in real life.

2. What suggestions did you find in the last section of the chapter for cultivating a character of peace? Which of these do you want to build into your life so as to make yourself a person who better reflects the Prince of Peace?

CHAPTER 7

HUMILITY *and* PRIDE

More than a thousand years have passed since the White Witch was defeated in the first Battle of Beruna, and Narnia is once again ruled by a cruel and unjust leader: the usurper Miraz. The rightful heir to the throne is thirteen-year-old Caspian, whose father was murdered by Miraz. Caspian's struggle to overthrow the false king is the subject of *Prince Caspian.* The War of Deliverance, as it comes to be known, culminates with the second Battle of Beruna, which takes place on the same site as the battle that saw the defeat of the White Witch in *The Lion, the Witch and the Wardrobe*. Following combat with the High King Peter, Miraz is killed by one of his own men, and his army is defeated. Aslan arrives on the scene, his presence sending fear throughout the ranks of Miraz' remaining soldiers but filling the hearts of talking beasts with joy. When Aslan asks if Caspian feels ready to become king of Narnia, Caspian replies that he doesn't think so. Aslan is pleased: "If you had felt yourself sufficient, it would have been a proof that you were not."[1] Humility is rewarded, and King Caspian begins his rule of Narnia with the blessing of Aslan.

Caspian's humility is exemplary. But in the Chronicles, even good characters exhibit pride at times. Many of them — including Jill Pole, Aravis, and the talking horse Bree — learn from their mistakes and grow in character. Unfortunately, other characters do not learn from their pride and so suffer the consequences. We will be looking at the range of prideful and humble attitudes in the Chronicles with an eye to how they reflect our own attitudes and what they teach us about how we ought to think about ourselves.

Pride is a temptation each of us struggles with in one way or another. Instead of recognizing that all of the good gifts we possess were given to us by God, we act as though we can take credit for them. Healthy self-respect crosses the line into arrogance. Striving to do better becomes selfish ambition. And along the way, our relationships with others and with God suffer (for who likes to be around a conceited person?). We set ourselves up for the letdown that will surely come when we are forced to face a more reasonable estimation of who we are. Even when we make progress in becoming humble, we can start to be proud of our humility! What are we to do?

It *is* possible to learn from our past mistakes of pride and to mature in character. We learn as much from the humbler characters of Narnia. According to C. S. Lewis's theory of ethics, good choices to act humbly, taken one after the other, can result in a character of true humility over time. But before we go any further with this line of thought, first we must ask ourselves a few basic questions. What is meant by *humility* and *pride*? How did Lewis use these terms?

A QUESTION OF COMPETITION

The concepts of humility and pride are familiar to us all. Yet as we examine them closely, we discover that they are more complex — and more interesting — than they at first may have appeared.

Humility is a quality that indicates a lack of pride, vanity, and conceit. It also connotes a kind of meekness or lowliness in position. It is not, however, the same as humiliation (feeling ashamed or diminished in an emotionally damaging sense). Lewis warned against making the wrong kinds of associations about the term *humility* and the humble person, who won't be what we expect. Lewis says our impressions of a humble person will likely be of a smart, optimistic person truly interested in what others have to say. The humble will not deliberately focus on humility or themselves at all.[2]

Lewis scholar Paul Ford associated humility with obedience, pointing out that *obedience* in the Latin sense (*oboedire*) means "to listen." "It is in this very specific sense that Lewis uses the word [obedience] in the *Chronicles*." Ford went on to define humility as "accepting and living in the truth of obedience" and gave the example of Caspian's humility before Aslan, as previously mentioned.[3]

By contrast, pride is associated with haughtiness, superiority, and arrogance. One dictionary defines pride in part as "a high or overweening opinion of one's own qualities . . . which gives rise to a feeling and attitude of superiority over and contempt for others."[4]

In a chapter in *Mere Christianity* titled "The Great Sin," Lewis condemned pride as "the essential vice, the utmost evil," viewing it as a vice that moves one to commit further acts of vice.[5] Lewis blamed much of the negativity resulting from pride on its inherently competitive nature, noting that when competition vanishes, so does pride. By competition, Lewis meant the need to have more than others, not just in the sense of material possessions, but also with regard to their talents (such as intelligence) or appearance (as in wanting to look better than others). Lewis also wrote that power is associated with pride. On the whole, pride is a creator of enmity, he observed, not only among human beings but also between creature and Creator. Pride is spiritually deadly. Like a disease, it devours the good.[6]

Lewis, however, also clarified misconceptions about pride. In *Mere Christianity*, he lists four misunderstandings. The first involves mistaken impressions of what a humble person may be like. Second, by pride Lewis did not mean the pleasure one gets from being rightly praised. The reason this is not pride, he said, is because the pleasure one derives from being praised in this manner is a result of rightly pleasing another. The focus, then, is not on oneself. There is, though, the potential for pride in such circumstances if the focus moves beyond the enjoyment of pleasing someone and begins to dwell on the achievements of the person being praised in such a way as to puff one up with pride. Third, Lewis noted that common statements that one is "proud" of things (such as one's school or military regiment) or of a person (such as a child) are not generally associated with the vice of pride. Instead, in such instances, "pride" really means admiration. Again, this kind of pride can lead to the vice of pride if taken in unhealthy directions, but it is better to be proud in this sense than it is to be proud of one's own abilities. Fourth, Lewis pointed out that pride should not be viewed as something forbidden by God because it offends Him. God, for instance, does not concern Himself with losing His dignity because of pride.[7] The focus of both pride as a vice and humility as a virtue is on the individual and how such attitudes impact one's relationship with God.

God puts pride and humility into proper perspective. Let us, then, turn next to what we may learn about pride and humility in the Bible.

BEFORE A FALL

The Bible speaks a great deal about humility and pride. As one theological dictionary observed, "The terminology for humility appears nearly a hundred times in the Bible, referencing multiple meanings."[8] For instance, Proverbs 16:18 reads,

> Pride goes before destruction,
> a haughty spirit before a fall.

And in a song of David we read,

> You save the humble,
> but your eyes are on the haughty to bring them low. (2 Samuel 22:28)

In the Bible, humility is used not only of human beings but also of God in the Incarnation:

> Being found in appearance as a man,
> [Christ] humbled himself
> and became obedient to death — even death
> on a cross! (Philippians 2:8)

Just prior to this passage, in verse 5, Paul states, "Your attitude should be the same as that of Christ Jesus," thus underscoring the importance of humility in the life of the Christian. Humility, for instance, is desirable when sharing the gospel (see 1 Peter 3:15). Although humility was considered a weakness, not a virtue, by the Greek culture at the time of the New Testament,[9] biblically speaking, humility *is* a virtue and is of particular importance for the individual's relationship to God. As the Creator, God is above His creatures, who should be humble before His awesome glory and presence.

To instead be filled with pride is to go against God and His character — to lift up oneself to a higher position than is called for. Pride is often condemned in the Bible. Lewis considered pride "the great sin" in part because of the pride of Satan that resulted in his downfall and also because of the pride of humanity exemplified by Adam and Eve. To strive against God out of arrogance is a serious matter; therefore, as warning, the Bible is replete with examples of this vice.

Nebuchadnezzar — king of Babylon from 605 to 562 BC — was proud of his rebuilding of Babylon, proclaiming, "Is not this the great Babylon I have built as the royal residence, by my mighty power and for the glory of my majesty?" (Daniel 4:30). In the next verse, we read, "The words were still on his lips when a voice came from heaven, 'This is what is decreed for you, King Nebuchadnezzar: Your royal authority has been taken from you.'" Although some have speculated that the enormous golden statue erected under the direction of Nebuchadnezzar was of the king himself, it is more likely that the statue was that of a god (see Daniel 3:1). Nevertheless, the king's pride is evident and the consequences of his behavior (namely insanity and the loss of his kingdom) are consistent with the biblical pattern of pride coming before a fall.

The New Testament also offers examples of pride, such as the downfall of Herod Agrippa. After this king delivered a speech, the people shouted, "This is the voice of a god, not of a man" (Acts 12:22). Following this comment, we read, "Immediately, because Herod did not give praise to God, an angel of the Lord struck him down, and he was eaten by worms and died" (Acts 12:23).

Referring to the nature of pride in the biblical view, the *Dictionary of Biblical Imagery* noted, "Pride keeps some very bad company. It is associated with such varied vices as perverted speech (Prov 8:13), boastfulness (Jer 48:30), defiance of God (Jer 50:29), indifference to the poor and needy (Ezek 16:49), self-deceit (Obad 3), the lust of the flesh and of the eyes (1 Jn 2:16) and false trust in riches (1 Tim 6:17). Twice pride is placed in a category of highly charged vices (Mk 7:21-22; 2 Tim 3:2-5)."[10] Pride infects an individual like a contagion, resulting in separation from God that can be healed only via humility leading to sincere repentance (see chapter 8).

In the Chronicles of Narnia, we see examples of humility that can guide us in our own attempts to avoid pride (and thus escape its consequences) and adopt humility (and thus receive its rewards).

Lowly in Narnia

Among the heroes and heroines of Narnia are men, women, and talking animals who possess such a true humility that they do not overestimate themselves or boast about their positions and accomplishments. Among them are royalty, great warriors, and other high achievers, and, therefore, they might naturally be proud, but they all have learned to make a reasonable estimate of themselves. Among these paragons of humility, the highest — and the unique one — is the great lion himself.

Aslan. Lewis did not intend Aslan to be an allegorical depiction of Christ in a strict sense.[11] Nevertheless, like Christ, Aslan offers the supreme example of humility. As Christ humbled Himself for our redemption, so too does Aslan humble himself to the point of death for the redemption of Edmund in *The Lion, the Witch and the Wardrobe*.[12] The act of the greater willingly becoming the lesser is an example of self-abasement. That Aslan continues to humble himself is made clear in *The Silver Chair* when, following the death of the elderly King Caspian, Aslan allows Eustace to wound him with a thorn so that the blood of the lion will revive and rejuvenate Caspian in Aslan's country.[13] Aslan allows himself to feel pain and give his blood for the eternal life of another.

Aslan is humble in another sense. While he is clearly a divine figure capable of performing the miraculous (such as the restoration of Reepicheep's tail in *Prince Caspian*), he allows lesser creatures to participate in his grand design for Narnia.[14] When, for instance, a magical apple is needed for the protection of Narnia in *The Magician's Nephew*, Aslan does not procure the apple himself, though he possesses the power to easily accomplish this task. Instead, he sends the young boy Digory Kirke, accompanied by his friend Polly Plummer and the winged horse Fledge. They encounter trials, and Digory is tempted by evil, but in the end the goal is accomplished and Digory grows in character. This is how it works for us, too, in the mystery of our participation with God.

In his essay "The Efficacy of Prayer," Lewis pondered the reason for petitionary prayer.[15] After all, if God is omnipotent, why does He command His followers to pray? In addressing this matter, Lewis quoted Blaise Pascal, who wrote that through prayer God imparts to His creatures "the dignity of causality."[16] God, like Aslan, does not *need* our prayers, but by His allowing us to pray, we commune with Him and are granted a certain dignity in knowing that we have participated in His plans. Similarly, God can accomplish other tasks for us, but He purposefully restrains Himself in order to allow us the dignity, joy, and sometimes pain required for us to grow as individuals and, in some limited sense, partake of God's majesty.[17]

Christians are not God's puppets or slaves but rather creatures whom He cares for—children He loves enough to humble Himself by becoming human and dying for us. Just as a human parent at times must step aside and let a child grow and learn on his or her own by attempting a task—even though the parent could accomplish the task quicker, easier, and often better than a child—so too does God humble Himself not because He is cruel and unjust but because He loves us and knows what is best for us.

Hwin. In *The Horse and His Boy*, Hwin is a talking Narnian mare captured as a foal and forced to live as a regular horse in Calormen. She is in the service of the young Tarkheena Aravis, but after she is forced to speak in order to prevent the suicide of Aravis, both agree to escape together and are fleeing to the North when they meet up with Shasta and Bree. Hwin is at times overly submissive and easily intimidated (particularly by the proud warhorse Bree), but on other occasions she humbly asserts herself. She is described as a gentle and nervous horse who is sometimes silenced and overruled by others.[18]

When Bree, Hwin, Aravis, and Shasta are making plans to travel through Tashbaan, Hwin is referred to as humble on two occasions. First, as the four are discussing plans to meet at ancient tombs on the other side of the city in case they become separated, Hwin humbly observes that the question at this stage is not what to do after they make it through the city but how they are to get through it in the first place. Later in the discussion, Shasta suggests that they will need to be disguised. Hwin adds that it would probably be safest to travel right through the city and blend in with the crowds. She suggests that the two humans dress in peasant rags and that both horses be made up as though they are pack animals. Although Bree's pride gets the better of him and he is concerned about arriving in Narnia in an unacceptable condition, Hwin is once again referred to as humble when she points out that their goal is to get to Narnia, implying that their appearance when they arrive is the least of their concerns.[19]

Shasta. The boy Shasta has lived his entire life as a peasant—really no more than a slave to a fisherman named Arsheesh, supposedly his father, who beats him at times.[20] Consequently, when Shasta overhears Arsheesh making plans to sell him as a slave and also learns that Arsheesh is not really his father, Shasta is eager to escape. He teams up with the talking horse Bree, and later they are joined by Aravis and Hwin. Perhaps because the only life he has known is one of a lowly peasant, Shasta is humble by nature. This may also explain his apparent indifference to Bree's pride in instances where Bree implies that Shasta is lowly compared to a great warhorse. Shasta is more sensitive to such implications when the pride of Aravis is contrasted with his peasant status, possibly because of his budding romantic interest in her. Shasta, however, thinks Aravis's pride is nonsensical.[21]

Shasta's humility is evident. Despite his courageous efforts to save Aravis and Hwin from an attack by a lion (discussed in chapter 2), he keeps this story to himself rather than brag about it. He wants the story told, but he has the humility to know that he should not be the one to tell it, and, in fact, when the story is told, Shasta is embarrassed by it.[22] Additionally, Shasta humbly admits that his part in the Battle of Anvard was minor. In response to Aravis's commenting that the battle must have been magnificent, Shasta replies that the battle was not what he anticipated, again avoiding an opportunity to exhibit pride.[23] When Shasta awkwardly reveals to Aravis that he is really Prince Cor of Archenland and is believed to have fulfilled a great prophecy, Aravis asks him if he feels proud.[24] Shasta (now Cor) humbly replies that he actually feels somewhat frightened.[25] Cor is also embarrassed when he appears before Aravis in his new princely clothing (he blushes). He quickly explains that he did not wear the clothes and bring a trumpeter to show off before her.[26]

Cor, future king of Archenland, exhibits a quality Aslan desires in leaders and in everyone else in Narnia: humility. And because Aslan represents God, his example shows that humility is a quality each of us ought to learn to possess. Some Narnian characters, however, display an attitude we are *not* to have.

All Puffed Up

The Chronicles of Narnia offer numerous examples of prideful characters. Among these is Reepicheep the mouse. When he loses his tail in the second Battle of Beruna, he shows signs of pride in his desire to have his tail back. In response, Aslan offers a mild chastisement, suggesting that Reepicheep focuses too much on matters of honor.[27]

Happily, Reepicheep's pride does not grow and become his undoing as it does in characters such as Prince Rabadash, King Miraz, and Jadis. The pride of Rabadash results in his being humbled by Aslan, who turns the troubled prince into a donkey for a time. King Miraz loses his throne at least partly as a result of his pride and foolish courage when he accepts an offer of combat against King Peter. After eating the forbidden fruit of Aslan, Jadis not only is physically more powerful but also has the appearance of pride.[28]

The examples of prideful characters could go on and on. Here, however, let us focus on three characters: Jill Pole, Aravis, and Bree.

Jill Pole. In *The Silver Chair*, Jill Pole, on her first visit to Narnia, is showing off at the edge of a cliff. Eustace Scrubb tries to stop Jill from getting too close to the edge. As Jill realizes the danger, she panics and Eustace falls off the edge. Fortunately, Eustace flies safely to Narnia on the breath of Aslan. In this incident, pride literally comes before a fall — the fall of Eustace as the result of the pride of Jill. Later, when Aslan asks her why she was so close to the edge of the cliff, Jill admits that she was being pretentious. Aslan commends her honest reply and instructs her not to behave in such a manner again. He also says that her task of finding Prince Rilian will be more trying as a result of her behavior at the cliff.[29] Pride has its consequences.

Not only does Jill have to live with the terrible memories of her prideful behavior (we are told she lived with these memories all her life — even in her dreams), she also must face the consequences of her actions by having to memorize the four signs Aslan gives her. The signs and the emphasis placed upon the memorization of them are an echo of biblical passages such as Deuteronomy 6:6-7, which says, "These commandments that I give you today are to be upon your hearts. Impress them on your children. Talk about them when you sit at home and when you walk along the road, when you lie down and when you get up." In *The Last Battle*, it is clear that Jill has grown in character. She expresses true humility when complimented on her archery skills and also displays courage in battle.[30]

Aravis. A Tarkheena of Calormen, Aravis is accustomed to a life of nobility and the respect and perks that come with it. Like her people as a whole, she is proud, but she begins to grow in character on her journey of escape from an arranged marriage to Ahoshta Tarkaan — described as an ugly old man who serves as the grand vizier to the Tisroc (the leader of the Calormen Empire).

Aravis underscores Lewis's belief that Christian transformation involves a process of reshaping one's character for the better over a period of time (Edmund and Eustace are two other examples of this). Her behavior upon first meeting Shasta indicates her initial pride. When Shasta notes that Aravis is merely a girl, Aravis retorts that Shasta is likely just a common slave boy and a thief who has taken the horse of his master. As the warhorse Bree continues to speak to the mare Hwin and not to her rider, Aravis is annoyed and asks about this behavior. Bree replies that Hwin is a free Narnian and, as such, is not her horse. In fact, Bree points out that he may as well refer to Aravis as Hwin's human — a comment that leaves Aravis speechless, likely because she realizes, for the first time, that things will be drastically different for her.[31] It is ironic that Aravis seems to address Bree the warhorse and not Bree's rider, Shasta, when she herself complains that Bree is not addressing her and is instead only speaking to Hwin the mare. It is not until later that Aravis begins to grow in humility as she realizes that in Narnia she will not be anyone particularly special.[32]

In her initial escape, Aravis also uses people for her ends, such as by convincing a servant to write a fraudulent letter and by drugging a maid. In the case of the maid, it is clear Aravis cares little for the punishment the girl might receive as a result of Aravis's ploy. Her pride blinds her to the consequences of her actions in the lives of others — a character flaw that is later corrected when she meets Aslan and learns that he was the lion who clawed her back in order that she might know the pain inflicted upon the drugged maid.[33]

Aravis, wearing peasant rags as a disguise, exhibits pride while preparing to enter the great city of Tashbaan. She comments to Shasta that because of her status, she should be traveling in style — the center of an entourage of soldiers and slaves, perhaps on her way to see the Tisroc.[34] Shasta is aware of the attitude Aravis conveys to him, noting that she believes she is better than he (because he is a peasant boy) and, hence, should not be traveling with him. She is described explicitly by the narrator as proud but also as loyal to her companions.[35]

In Tashbaan, Shasta is separated from the others, and Aravis meets her friend the Tarkheena Lasaraleen, who is now married and of high position. In some ways, Lasaraleen represents what Aravis must have been like herself: proud, vain, self-centered, and a gossip. The flighty Lasaraleen expresses disdain over Aravis's traveling with a peasant, prompting Aravis to respond with a hint of humility that she, too, will be unknown in Narnia.[36]

Her time with the Hermit of the Southern March brings further improvements in Aravis's character. Shasta's courage in facing what he believed to be a wild lion in order to help Aravis and Hwin is sobering for Aravis. She recognizes she has been treating him as lower than herself, but now Shasta has proven himself to be a courageous and caring individual.[37] Her encounter with Aslan also has a powerful effect on her, as she realizes her maid was punished severely as a result of her actions. In short, she begins to think of others more than of herself — an important step on the road to humility. Aravis appears to have learned an important lesson and, setting aside her pride, ultimately apologizes to Shasta.[38]

In the end, though Aravis is humbled, she is rewarded when she becomes queen of Archenland as a result of her marriage to

Cor. This brings to mind the biblical passage "Humble yourselves before the Lord, and he will lift you up" (James 4:10). Humble Christians are not guaranteed positions of royalty during their earthly lives, but the Bible does speak of heavenly rewards of different kinds, even using words such as "crowns" to describe them (see 1 Corinthians 9:25; 2 Timothy 4:8; James 1:12; 1 Peter 5:4; Revelation 2:10; 3:11). Of course, one should not become a Christian for rewards but because Christianity is "true and reasonable" (Acts 26:25).

Bree. Like Hwin, Bree was captured as a foal and taken to Calormen.[39] As a result, he is forced to live as though he were a witless beast. He is distinguished as a warhorse, which, combined with his many years of captivity in Calormen, no doubt contributes to his pride. He knows he is better than the dumb horses, and being the warhorse of a Tarkaan, he is raised in an environment conducive to pride. His intelligence naturally contributes to his success in battle, especially in comparison with dumb beasts. Still, he longs for Narnia and the North, and when he sees his chance for escape, he takes it.[40]

That Bree thinks much of himself and often thinks little of others is immediately clear. He knows his chances of escape with the boy Shasta are better than if he were to go alone, but he thinks poorly of him. When he asks Shasta if he can ride and the boy replies that he has ridden a donkey, Bree responds contemptuously, obviously looking down on both the donkey and Shasta. Bree tells Shasta that he is not to hold the reins or grab the horse's mane because Bree will be in control the entire time — another indication of his take-charge pride. Bree obviously thinks it beneath him to have a peasant boy riding him, comparing the boy to a sack of potatoes. Later Bree remarks that it would be shameful to be seen with Shasta on a main road. Bree indicates that he looks down on horses who pull chariots and that he views cavalry horses, such as himself, as superior — yet another indication of his pride.[41]

Bree's vanity (a form of pride) is clear in at least two instances. First, although he enjoys rolling in grass, he is concerned that such behavior may not be proper in Narnia. When Shasta laughs at his actions, Bree is genuinely perturbed. Shasta tells him that he really shouldn't worry about it, as the important thing is to get to Narnia. Second, Bree is overly concerned about his appearance. When Hwin suggests the horses be made to look like pack animals, cutting their tails as part of the disguise, Bree is concerned about arriving in Narnia with a ragged tail. Hwin replies (echoing the words of Shasta regarding the matter of rolling in the grass) that the real goal is simply to arrive in Narnia.[42]

In one amusing segment of the story involving the proud giving advice to the proud, Bree offers suggestions to Aravis as to how she should carry herself in order to come across as a peasant. But when Aravis offers Bree advice on how to look less like a warhorse, Bree tells her to be silent.[43]

When Bree, Hwin, Aravis, and Shasta are running from a lion, Shasta shows courage by jumping off Bree and turning back to help. This incident has a powerful impact on Bree, who does not feel worthy of entering Narnia because he fled when Shasta did the right thing. He is shamed (though not quite humbled in the proper sense) because he, a warhorse, has been bested by a boy.[44]

It will take more than his reflecting on the incident to truly change Bree for the better. First, the Hermit tells Bree that if he really is humble, then he needs to be sensible, adding that Bree is not as great as he thinks he is and probably will not stand out in any particular way when he reaches Narnia. If Bree knows this, he'll be on the right path to becoming a proper horse. Next, an encounter with Aslan nudges Bree further in the direction of humility. While he is explaining in a condescending manner to Aravis that Aslan is not a lion in a literal sense, Aslan bounds over the wall, and as one of his whiskers tickles Bree's ear, the horse gallops away in fear.[45] Confirming Bree's primary character flaw, Aslan calls him proud and beckons him to experience Aslan by touch and smell in order to prove that the lion is really a beast.[46]

Bree and other Narnian characters prove that there is hope for the prideful — and that includes you and me.

Overcoming the Great Sin

Apologist Josh McDowell observed that one of the three common causes for the rejection of Christ is being prideful (the other two are being ignorant of truth and having a moral problem).[47] Not only is pride an obstacle to belief (and repentance), but pride is also a problem in the life of the Christian. Lewis considered pride the great sin because it not only leads to other vices but also creates enmity with God. It is accurately labeled, in Lewis's words, a spiritual cancer. Sustained pride is accompanied by consequences. Those who think of themselves as better than they are will eventually become arrogant and their pride will grow. But as pride increases, the quality of one's relationship with God declines.

Humility, on the other hand, allows room for God to move in one's life and enables one to be more open to God's leading. Hwin's submissive and humble character, for instance, prompts her to boldly approach Aslan despite her obvious fear. As she approaches Aslan, she notes his beauty and offers herself to be eaten by him. She is rewarded by Aslan, who kisses her on the nose and tells her that she will have joy.[48] Similarly, God wants us to seek Him humbly, realizing He is the Creator. In *Mere Christianity,* Lewis said that in order for a person to be humble, "the first step is to realize that one is proud."[49] We should not wait for an ethical crisis in order to cultivate humility in our lives; instead, we must daily strive for humility and be on guard against the vice of pride.

As we attempt to remain vigilant against pride, we should remember that pride can manifest itself in not only our external behavior but also our internal disposition. We may, for instance, outwardly appear humble while we are inwardly thriving on pride. Spiritual pride, too, is a danger.

One way to combat pride is to study the many biblical passages that offer insights on the topic (several such passages were touched upon earlier in this chapter). But we must do more than simply read passages passively. We must strive to first understand what the Bible says about humility and pride and then make an effort to apply it to our lives regularly and meaningfully. Moreover, Christ must be the center of our focus, including a sincere desire to emulate His character in order to grow in virtue. As Paul wrote, "Your attitude should be the same as that of Christ Jesus" (Philippians 2:5), referring to Jesus' humbling of Himself, so we must, through the power of the Holy Spirit, strive to avoid the vice of pride and to humble ourselves.

Reflection and Response Questions

1. The four main characters of *The Horse and His Boy* — Shasta, Aravis, Hwin, and Bree — show us different shades of humility and pride. In terms of the vice/virtue pair of pride and humility, which of the four characters do you think you resemble the most? Why?

2. Pride is such an insidious vice that nearly all of us struggle with it one way or another. We may be proud of our looks, intelligence, achievements, wealth, or talents — even our presumed humility! In what area do you struggle the most with pride, and how can you root out that type of pride from your life?

3. What forms can false humility take? What would true humility look like in your life? (For ideas about pursuing Christlike humility, look up these passages: Matthew 5:5; 20:20-28; 23:11-12; Mark 10:13-16; Luke 14:7-11; John 5:30; 13:4-15; James 2:1-10.)

Chapter 8

Repentance *and* Unrepentance

In *The Lion, the Witch and the Wardrobe,* when Tumnus the faun brings Lucy Pevensie to his home, he kindly offers her tea and snacks, tells her about Narnia, and plays his flute for her. Then, to Lucy's astonishment, Tumnus begins to cry in great sobs as though his heart is broken. He turns to the portrait of his father hanging above the mantelpiece and guiltily says that the older faun would not have behaved as Tumnus has. Her host admits to Lucy that he has brought her to his home intending to turn her over to the White Witch, who rules Narnia. The witch has ordered him to bring her any human he might meet, and Tumnus has no doubt that she would treat cruelly any human captive. But now he realizes how wicked it would be to deliver this innocent child to the witch, and so he cannot go through with his plan. Rather than turning Lucy over to the witch, he guides her back to the lamppost in the woods, where she is able to find her way back to England via the open wardrobe door.[1]

Tumnus repents of his evil intentions. In this, Tumnus offers a model for us when we have done wrong by word, thought, or deed. Each of us is fallen and separated from God, and if a person is to be saved from ultimate judgment, he or she must reach a key point of repentance and faith in Jesus Christ. But even those who have gone through that kind of repentance still need to repent whenever they sin. Like Tumnus, we realize in repentance that we have not lived up to the standard set before us, and we become truly sorry for it and change our ways.

As we face the daily temptations in our lives and sometimes give in to them, repentance is a skill we need to learn. The more responsive we become to conviction about our wrongdoing, the easier we find repentance to be. This is another way that a godly character may be developed over time through a series of good choices.

But, specifically speaking, what is repentance and what is unrepentance? Moreover, how do they relate to ethics and, in particular, to the Christian worldview?

BEYOND "I'M SORRY"

Repentance is often defined as a feeling of regret over wrongdoing. Contrition is usually included in the definition, as in feeling sincerely and deeply sorry. Repentance involves remorse over one's conduct and, as such, it encompasses morality.[2]

If there is no right and wrong, then logically one need never repent. But in the real world, even if the term *repentance* is not used, everyone is aware that the need to apologize (or be apologized to) is a fact of human nature. Apologizing and genuinely meaning it is a form of repentance. Lewis said that repentance is not enjoyable—that it involves retraining behavior centered on the self, and that true repentance involves the death of a part of oneself.[3] This is much more than saying, "I'm sorry," because Lewis, of course, was attempting to describe true repentance within the framework of Christianity.

To Lewis, it made sense that those who know they need to repent must first have an understanding of moral law and the fact there is a personal moral Lawgiver behind such standards. Otherwise, they would not know that repentance, followed by forgiveness, is needed, and Christianity would be meaningless to them. There may be practical, atheistic, or humanistic reasons for repentance, such as for the purposes of getting along in a community, but Lewis would not view such forms of repentance as based on a firm foundation, and certainly he would not view them as having the kind of scope and power involved in Christian repentance.

One who is unrepentant does not express sorrow over sin, ask forgiveness, or see a need for a radical change of mind and behavior. A murderer who expresses no remorse for his crime is obviously unrepentant. But unrepentance need not be evident only in extreme situations. Everyday life provides opportunities for right and wrong behavior and, as a result, for unrepentance or repentance.

Unrepentance comes in at least two forms. First, a person who appears outwardly unrepentant may in fact not believe repentance is necessary. This person actually must have some inherent sense of right and wrong and, consequently, knows deep down inside that he or she has done wrong, but this person obscures the knowledge. Second, a person may blatantly display unrepentance despite being aware of the wrongdoing. This person is more culpable than the first because of his or her clear knowledge of wrongdoing (though both are accountable).

Whether or not the inherent nature of human beings, created in God's image and capable of grasping moral law to some extent, can be abolished is an interesting question and one grappled with to some extent by Lewis in *The Abolition of Man*.[4] As discussed in the next section, people do have special revelation (the Bible) and, as such, are accountable to the standards it provides as well as the repentance-based remedy it offers—a remedy that the unrepentant choose to reject.

THE U-TURN OF REPENTANCE

Matthew 4:17 reads, "Jesus began to preach, 'Repent, for the kingdom of heaven is near.'" Repentance, thus, stretches back to the very beginning of the Christian message. Indeed, both the Old and New Testaments have much to say about repentance and its role in the process of regeneration, which leads to biblical salvation.

Many scholars have noted the importance of Psalm 51 in relation to repentance. Gordon Lewis and Bruce Demarest, for example, noted six aspects of repentance outlined by David the psalmist in the passage: "David expressed *awareness of his sins* (vv. 1-3).... He offered heart-felt *confession of sins* (vv. 4-5).... [He] showed a true *attitude of contrition*.... He uttered a *prayer for pardon of sins* (vv. 7-9) [that is, he sought forgiveness].... [He] sought profound *inner renewal* (vv. 10-12).... David experienced the joy that comes from deliverance from sin and its consequences (v. 12)."[5] The *Dictionary of*

Biblical Imagery notes four broad aspects of repentance as contained in the psalm: "comprehension of wrong done, earnest desire for justice, desire for the presence of God, and changed action."[6]

Biblical repentance calls for a radical change of mind. As the apostle Paul noted, "Godly sorrow brings repentance that leads to salvation and leaves no regret, but worldly sorrow brings death" (2 Corinthians 7:10). But this godly sorrow must be combined "with a resolution to turn from [sin]."[7] Consequently, repentance encompasses a moral dimension. In order to turn away from wrong behavior, one must first have knowledge of a standard of right behavior.

Moreover, repentance, though an important step in the process of redemption, need not in and of itself lead to salvation. One may repent, but maybe not to the point of the godly sorrow that leads to salvation. Someone may also repent simply because of circumstances, such as Uncle Andrew does in *The Magician's Nephew*. Though we are told that after his trying experiences with Jadis and the talking creatures of Narnia he became a better person, no clear indication of sincere repentance is given.[8]

Examples of unrepentance appear throughout the Bible. The fallen angel referred to as Satan or Lucifer, for instance, is clearly unrepentant (see Revelation 12:7-9). Israel, as a whole, was often unrepentant, causing a number of prophets to call the nation to repentance.

Lewis was more concerned with the need for individual repentance and, in fact, wrote an essay on the dangers of national repentance. In his essay, he voiced concerns over national repentance, such as failing to repent of our own sins because we are so focused on the sins of others (for example, some actions taken by government leaders). In other words, Lewis was concerned that national repentance would detract from the more important need of personal repentance.[9]

The moral factor involved in repentance and unrepentance cannot be underestimated. In order for one to be truly repentant, one must be humble, have an understanding of mercy, be honest regarding the behavior that requires repentance, have some understanding of justice, and possess the courage to face one's wrongdoings and take responsibility for them. The unrepentant, on the other hand, are characterized by pride and are dishonest about the nature and extent of their behavior.[10]

Repentant characters in the Chronicles exhibit an understanding of the wrong they have done and are willing to show their repentance by their changed actions. The unrepentant characters, however, imprison themselves in their own willful blindness, effectively cutting themselves off from truth.

While insights and parallels to biblical repentance and unrepentance can be drawn from the Chronicles, it must be remembered that Lewis did not write the stories as systematic theology. As a result, while characters exhibit qualities of repentance, Lewis was not attempting to present deep theological reflections on the topic. Nevertheless, his examples of repentance and unrepentance are instructive, as careful readers will gain from them a better understanding of the relevance of these matters in their own lives.

REMORSEFUL IN NARNIA

Narnia, in some respects, represents our own world. There are wicked people within it, but most people do not appear overtly evil. However, the Bible teaches that there is a serious problem with the human condition as it is—a problem that is in need of radical redemption and salvation. Fortunately, Lewis presented several examples of repentance in the Chronicles that each of us can learn from.

Tumnus. As we have already seen, the behavior of Tumnus the faun toward Lucy represents repentance.[11] His weeping shows his contrition (that is, his deep sorrow) over his plans to kidnap Lucy and hand her over to the White Witch. It should be noted, however, that such an emotional display need not necessarily accompany true repentance. Lewis himself, for instance, described his point of accepting Christ as not being a particularly emotional event (he described it as realizing he was awake after being asleep for a long time).[12]

Nevertheless, the behavior of Tumnus, combined with other factors, indicates true repentance. First, Tumnus is aware that his intention to kidnap Lucy is wrong. Second, he confesses this fact. Third, he is contrite about the situation. Fourth, he asks forgiveness from Lucy. Fifth, Tumnus acts on his repentance by guiding Lucy back to the lamppost. Sixth, Tumnus realizes that even though he is repentant, there may be consequences to his actions.

That final aspect of Tumnus's repentance is perhaps especially instructive for us. Tumnus describes a number of ways the White Witch may punish him if she finds out he has come across a human and let the human go.[13] In fact, Tumnus is later captured and turned to stone by the witch. This goes to show that Christian repentance does not mean freedom from the consequences of one's actions, but it does mean that one has made a conscious effort and a radical change that, in light of eternity, is worth it.

Edmund. Unlike the emotional display of Tumnus, the repentance of Edmund is subtler and intertwined with his redemption by Aslan and the boy's subsequent changed behavior. Recall that in *The Lion, the Witch and the Wardrobe,* Edmund betrays his brother and sisters to the White Witch. He is in need of repentance not only for this despicable act but also for his behavior prior to his visit to Narnia. It seems that for some time, Edmund has been a bully.[14] Upon first meeting the witch, Edmund is quickly taken in by her false kindness and offer of Turkish Delight, which he greedily devours. His moral decline no doubt contributes to his subsequent betrayal.

After Edmund is rescued from the witch, who was going to sacrifice him, he spends some time with Aslan. Lewis did not reveal what Aslan and Edmund discuss, but he did note that it was a conversation Edmund remembers all his life.

Edmund's only recorded words indicating repentance are his brief apology to Peter, Susan, and Lucy. But Edmund's drastic change of heart is also revealed by his actions, particularly his bravery during the Battle of Beruna, in which he courageously attacks the White Witch and breaks her wand — a pivotal action in the battle. Lucy heals the wounded Edmund with her magical potion and notes that his appearance is much improved and that he has not looked so well for a long time.[15] Edmund's change is confirmed by Aslan, who makes the boy a knight.

Although Lucy and Susan discuss whether they should tell Edmund about Aslan's sacrifice on his behalf, the outcome of their discussion is not given.[16] However, because Edmund grows up to be more solemn than his brother, is known as King Edmund the Just, and indicates his understanding that Aslan saved him, it is reasonable to suppose that somehow he learned of Aslan's sacrifice.[17] In any event, Edmund understands what it is to be a traitor, and, more important, he understands what it means to be a traitor who has experienced repentance.

Eustace. Eustace Clarence Scrubb makes his first appearance in *The Voyage of the "Dawn Treader,"* an adventure in which he experiences redemption and a form of repentance leading to marked improvements in his character. On what is later termed Dragon Island, Eustace's desire to avoid work leads him to stray from his companions.[18] Eustace witnesses the death of a dragon, finds the cave of the dead dragon, and carefully enters. When he discovers vast amounts of treasure inside, Eustace's thoughts turn to greed. He begins to think it would not be so bad to be stuck in this world, so long as he has wealth. Eustace then falls asleep upon the dragon's treasure. Lewis specifically noted that because Eustace sleeps on the treasure with thoughts of greed, he is transformed into a dragon.[19] In short, Eustace's exterior appearance (that of a dragon) now matches his inward behavior and disposition.

Upon realizing his transformation, Eustace (after an initial thought of revenge) also realizes he desires the friendship and companionship of others, but he is struck with a terrible feeling of aloneness. He realizes, too, that the others had not treated him as badly as he had thought and that, in fact, he had not been as nice as he had considered himself to be. After he is able to communicate to the others that he has been transformed into a dragon and offers assistance to them, everyone notices his improved behavior. While he is a dragon, Eustace learns the joys of being helpful and realizes that he has been troublesome.[20] In so doing, Eustace's acknowledgment of his sinful behavior exhibits an aspect of repentance.

But there are still several more steps in his process of repentance, including inner renewal, which he experiences in a profound way when he meets Aslan for the first time. We learn of Eustace's encounter by way of his conversation with Edmund, the first person to see Eustace after he has become a boy again. Edmund is the perfect choice for Eustace to discuss the matter with because Edmund also has experienced the redemption of Aslan.

Eustace explains that Aslan came to him and led him to a high mountain, where he saw a deep well of clear, bubbling water. Eustace was eager to enter the water, but Aslan told him that he must undress first. At first Eustace did not understand because in dragon form he wore no clothes. But then it became clear that he was to shed his skin. Three times Eustace did this, but still his skin was as scaly and rough as before. Aslan explained that Eustace must let the lion undress him, and though the first tear of the lion's claws was deep and painful, the experience was also pleasurable. Eustace noticed that the skin Aslan tore off was considerably thicker than the skins he was able to remove on his own, signifying the profound nature of sin and wretchedness in the human condition that can be cured by only God. Then Aslan picked Eustace up and threw him into the water (an allusion to Christian baptism). After a time, Aslan took Eustace out of the water and clothed him. Eustace then exhibits another quality of repentance by apologizing for his past behavior and acknowledging that he had behaved poorly. Edmund tells Eustace about Aslan, the savior of Edmund as well as of all Narnia.[21]

While Lewis believed there is indeed a defining moment of repentance in the life of every true Christian, he also viewed repentance as an ongoing process thereafter (or at least one that will continue until our final state). In this vein, he observed that Eustace begins to change but still has relapses. Still, as Lewis put it, "The cure had begun."[22]

The enigma of Emeth. The character Emeth, featured in *The Last Battle*, presents something of an enigma when it comes to repentance and redemption. This is especially true for evangelical Christians, who tend to adhere to the particularist position of salvation (that is, only those who hear of Christ in this life and follow Him are saved).[23]

Emeth—whose name means "truth" in Hebrew—is a Calormene soldier and a follower of the false god Tash.[24] He is skeptical of the so-called Tashlan concocted by Shift the ape and Rishda Tarkaan and boldly enters the stable door so that he can meet Tash.[25] After defending himself against the attack of a Calormene soldier within the stable, Emeth finds himself in Aslan's country. What is puzzling is that even though Emeth has been an ardent follower of the false god Tash, Aslan explains that all of the devotion Emeth has given to Tash has really been to

Aslan; therefore, Emeth is allowed to enter Aslan's country.[26]

Before addressing the question of Emeth further, we should note that Lewis was by no means a religious pluralist (that is, one who believes that everyone will be saved, all roads lead to God, and so on).[27] This is evident from Lewis's belief in repentance. After all, why repent if God accepts you no matter what? But Lewis's position on pluralism is even clearer in another scene in *The Last Battle* that parallels in many ways the biblical scene of Christ's judgment, namely the scene in which some enter Aslan's country and others are turned away.[28] That's not the portrayal we would expect from a pluralist.

Another passage proving that Lewis was no pluralist is found in *The Silver Chair*. Jill Pole is thirsty, but she is afraid to approach a stream because of the presence of Aslan there.[29] At one point in the discussion between the girl and the lion, Jill asks if there is another stream to drink from, and Aslan soberly replies that this is the only stream.[30] His response can be interpreted as emphasizing Lewis's belief that Christ is the only one who can satisfy spiritual thirst.

Rejecting particularism and pluralism, Lewis settled on what he likely considered the middle ground, known as inclusivism. This position essentially asserts that "although God saves people only on the merits of Christ, not all who are saved have consciously known of Jesus or heard the gospel."[31] Based on the revelation they have, some people respond to God in such a way that God honors their devotion. As a result, Emeth, who has presumably never had an opportunity to learn clearly about Aslan, is nevertheless devout and faithful within the belief system available to him, and, therefore, Aslan accepts this devotion.

In *Mere Christianity,* Lewis observed that God has not revealed to us the details of how He will deal with those who have not heard the gospel. He stresses, though, what God *has* revealed to us, namely that salvation is only through Christ and that the more important question is what one who knows about the gospel will do in response.[32] Later, Lewis wrote that God leads some people involved in a non-Christian religion to focus on aspects of their religion that agree with Christian doctrines. Such people, noted Lewis, unknowingly are Christ's.[33] In a letter Lewis wrote that he believed God accepts prayers to other gods and that Jesus will save a number of individuals who are unaware that they are serving Christ. Lewis offered the parable of the sheep and the goats in Matthew 25:31-46 (wherein some of the "sheep" do not understand when they had served Christ) as his defense of this position.[34]

Winfried Corduan, commenting on the case of Emeth, wrote, "By implication, service to a pagan deity — again restricted to only those deeds done with truth and integrity — is implicit service to God." Corduan added, "The problem with this scenario is that it simply never occurs in the Bible."[35]

However one interprets Lewis's inclusivism as depicted by Emeth, it seems that Lewis did not believe such cases are common. Emeth, after all, is only one Calormene among presumably thousands (since Calormen is a vast empire) who is allowed entry into Aslan's country.[36] However, Emeth does appear to have a change of mind, as he speaks highly of Aslan later when he is telling the story to others.[37] This sets him apart from the unrepentant Calormenes as well as from all the other unrepentant characters in the Chronicles of Narnia.

Stiff-Necked in Narnia

Some of the most dislikable characters in the Chronicles portray for us what unrepentance looks like. While unrepentance itself may be appealing (we don't like to admit we are wrong; we prefer to do things our own way), these examples show us just what unrepentance really adds up to.

The White Witch. Jadis possesses a number of moral shortcomings that result in unrepentance. She is proud, cruel, dishonest, unfair, and warlike. In *The Magician's Nephew*, Jadis makes it clear that she is not willing to yield to anyone or anything, even when she is defeated. Thus, she utters the Deplorable Word, destroying her world, and never expresses remorse over this incident. She freely breaks (or, more aptly, ignores) rules, such as when she climbs the wall into Aslan's garden to eat a forbidden fruit.[38] In *The Lion, the Witch and the Wardrobe*, she has made it winter in Narnia for a hundred years and shows no signs of repentance over the cruelty she has wreaked upon the creatures and the land. She makes a show of respecting the Deep Magic only when it suits her purpose of disposing of Aslan and regaining control of Narnia. She is driven by greed and its accompanying desire for power. The core of her problem is that of humanity as described in the Bible — the desire to be God, or at least like God (see Genesis 3). Her vices blind her to the need for repentance.

Prince Rabadash. The eldest son of the Tisroc of Calormen, Rabadash seeks to marry Queen Susan of Narnia. When Susan decides to reject the marriage proposal and she and the other Narnians flee Tashbaan out of fear of what Rabadash might do, Rabadash is infuriated and his pride is hurt. He convinces his father to allow him to launch an attack on Anvard, a stronghold of Narnia's neighbor and ally Archenland. Rabadash and his army are defeated.

When King Lune of Archenland is considering how to punish Rabadash, the prince most plainly displays his unrepentance. If Rabadash were thinking clearly instead of being driven by rage, he would perhaps have accepted Lune's gracious offer, suggested by Queen Lucy, to let him go so long as he promises not to behave in such a manner again. Instead, Rabadash is clearly unrepentant, cutting off the king in midsentence and calling him names. As Rabadash ends his tirade, the king once again offers the prince a chance to accept his offer, but Rabadash replies that he does not wish to hear the terms and threatens Narnia and Archenland with further attacks.[39]

Aslan appears in the midst of the gathering, urges Rabadash to accept the terms offered, and warns him that another judgment is near if he does not. Aslan tells the prince to forget his pride and anger and to instead receive the compassion offered him. But the impenitence of the prince is deep, and he responds with another tirade, this time foolishly directed at Aslan (the prince calls the lion names).[40] The lion is still willing to extend mercy and an opportunity for repentance, but Rabadash will have none of it. Aslan then transforms Rabadash (albeit temporarily) into a donkey. Still, Rabadash exhibits no repentance. He does not show an awareness of his wrong behavior and, as a result, sees no need to confess his wrongdoings. Neither is Rabadash contrite; he expresses no interest in seeking pardon or renewal.

The dwarfs. Whereas Rabadash is impetuous and unrepentant from his first appearance in *The Horse and His Boy* to his last, the dwarfs in *The Last Battle* appear to have followed a progression that ultimately leads to their unrepentance. (The notable exceptions in their number are two dwarfs: Poggin, who leaves the renegade dwarfs to join King Tirian and his party, and an unnamed dwarf who, although a member of the group of troublesome dwarfs, is allowed to enter Aslan's country.)[41]

The story of the unrepentant dwarfs occurs in three sections. First, some thirty dwarfs who are prisoners of four Calormene soldiers encounter Tirian, who is disguised as a Tarkaan, and his companions, Eustace, Jill, Jewel, and Puzzle. Tirian eagerly reveals that the so-called Aslan they have been shown by Shift the ape was really a fraud (it's Puzzle wearing a lion's skin) and that Tirian has come to rescue the dwarfs so they can free Narnia. Unfortunately, the dwarfs are fed up with stories about Aslan. Their hearts have hardened to the point of extreme skepticism. Through their primary spokesperson, Griffle the dwarf, they say they are no longer interested in kings or Aslan or nonsensical tales.[42] Then, uttering a refrain that repeats five times throughout the book, they reply, "The Dwarfs are for the Dwarfs," thus emphasizing their self-centeredness and desire to separate themselves from Narnia.[43] Only Poggin leaves the group and joins Tirian and his companions.

The second section featuring the dwarfs occurs during the last battle against the Calormene soldiers, Tirian, and Tirian's companions. Here the dwarfs mock the Calormene forces and are given another opportunity by Tirian to repent of their traitorous actions, as he urges them to return to the side of Narnia. But they will have none of it. In fact, they consider Tirian's forces to be as bad as the Calormenes.[44] Upon seeing the arrival of reinforcements in the form of a group of talking horses coming to the aid of Tirian, the dwarfs begin to fire their arrows, killing all of the horses, thus committing one more act of treachery requiring repentance. Not long after, the remaining dwarfs (about eleven) are thrown through the stable door, which leads to the third and final appearance of the dwarfs.

Although the dwarfs are now in Aslan's country, they believe they have been thrown into a filthy, dark stable. Lucy has tried to help them but has failed. She asks Tirian, who has just come through the stable door himself, to try to talk some sense into them. The dwarfs, who are sitting in a circle, can hear the approach of the others but cannot see them even though it is daylight. When Lucy offers flowers to a dwarf named Diggle so he can smell that he is not in a stable, he believes he is smelling the sort of trash and filth one might find in a stable.[45] When Tirian grabs Diggle in order to pull him out of the circle and prove the dwarf is not in a stable, the dwarf behaves as though he has been hit against a wall and rushes back to the circle.

Only when Lucy asks Aslan to help the unrepentant dwarfs is some explanation of their condition offered. When Aslan growls near the dwarfs, they think it is a machine the others are using to trick them. Aslan then creates a feast for the dwarfs, but they do not see it as a feast and shortly begin to fight over who has the best bits of food. Aslan explains that the dwarfs will not allow themselves to be helped because they have opted for their own perceived cleverness rather than being open to believing in Aslan. They have mentally imprisoned themselves and are so fearful of being duped that nothing can reach them.[46]

Aslan's words echo one of Lewis's comments in *The Great Divorce* regarding hell as a choice. Lewis wrote of two types of people. The first humbly allow God's will to be done, but in the case of the second group of people, God allows *their* will to be done.[47] In other words, they choose to live separately from God, and He grants their wish for all eternity: hell.

May none of us be a part of that second group. May we always seek God's will to be done, and that involves repenting of doing things sinfully our own way.

A CHOICE TO MAKE

Pride and other vices cloud one's perceptions and obscure the need for repentance. The longer one's actions are moving in a negative direction, compounded by sins small and great, the more difficult it becomes to turn to God with the sorrow and contrition required for salvation.

Lewis observed that for those who have sincerely repented of their wrongdoings and embraced the gospel of Christ, repentance must continue throughout life. Just as Eustace repents and gets on the right track and yet still needs to apologize at times, so the need for repentance is ongoing in the Christian life.[48] Those who grow more distant from God and an understanding of their fallen condition and need for repentance separate themselves from truth by their own perceived cleverness. That's what happens with the dwarfs in *The Last Battle.* Their extreme skepticism and materialistic worldview has blinded them and imprisoned them and resulted in a hardening of the heart.

While the character of Emeth presents an interesting theological case study, bringing up questions of religious inclusivism, it should be noted that beyond the academic study of why Emeth is allowed to enter Aslan's country even though the Calormenes believed in Tash, the question of what we will do with the gospel of Christ as it has been revealed to us is of utmost importance. As Christ asked His disciples, "What about you? Who do you say I am?" (Matthew 16:15). Our answer to that high-stakes question will result in our becoming, as Lewis put it, either "immortal horrors" in a hell of our own choosing or "everlasting splendours" in the presence of God.[49] The Bible says that God sent His Son, Jesus Christ, to suffer and die for our sins, but His resurrection signified His conquering of sin and an opportunity for each of us to come to Him on His terms, with sincere repentance.

What is *your* answer to the question posed by Christ? As 2 Peter 3:9 reads, God "is patient with you, not wanting anyone to perish, but everyone to come to repentance." But God will not wait forever. One day this world will end; it will be too late to repent then. As Lewis wrote, "Now, today, this moment, is our chance to choose the right side. . . . We must take it or leave it."[50]

Although the Holy Spirit lives within Christians, we still possess a fallen nature that at times leads us to sin in thought, word, or deed. When this occurs, we must humbly turn to God, confessing our sins with sincere repentance. On a practical level, it may be helpful for us to establish some sort of accountability structure with one or more trusted friends in order to keep us on track in this regard and assist with spiritual growth.

We also need to keep in mind the seriousness of repentance

before a holy God. Too often, Christians fail to understand how actions that require repentance not only are harmful to the individual and to people one has sinned against but also are an affront to God. As Jerry Bridges observed, "Our first problem is that *our attitude toward sin is more self-centered than God-centered.* We are more concerned about our own 'victory' over sin than we are about the fact that our sins grieve the heart of God."[51] When we have grieved God by our sin, only repentance will restore the broken relationship with Him.

In the Chronicles of Narnia, Lucy is the human character closest to Aslan, and because of this she is well attuned to his expectations. When Lucy sins and is in need of repentance, Aslan merely needs to growl or look at her in order for her to understand not only that she has sinned but also that she has grieved the heart of Aslan.[52] So, too, we must cultivate our relationship with God to the point where we are attuned to His expectations and, as a result, know almost instinctively when we are in need of repentance and have grieved the heart of God. The moral choices we make over time will either help us become more attuned to virtue and, hence, to the need for repentance or dull our moral senses to the point of confusion and the distancing of ourselves from God and His grace.

Reflection and Response Questions

1. Review the story of Tumnus and Lucy, as summarized at the beginning of this chapter. What do you find in Tumnus's

repentance that provides a helpful model for your own repentance for wrongdoing?

2. Spend some time soul searching. Does your conscience convict you of unconfessed sin in your life? Tell God you are sorry for your wrongdoing, and ask for His help to reform your life in areas in which you have sinned.

3. Of all that you have learned from reading this book, what insight do you think God would most want you to carry with you so that it may change your life?

Conclusion

The Chronicles of Narnia are rich, imaginative works brimming with practical insights that touch upon matters of great importance. This accounts for their continuing popularity decades after their initial publication. The Chronicles also endure because they reflect the character and commitment of a man, C. S. Lewis, who was filled with a sense of wonder and longing for joy that is elusive unless it is found in the King of kings and Lord of lords (see 1 Timothy 6:15; Revelation 17:14; 19:16). As Augustine wrote, "our hearts find no peace until they rest" in God.[1]

In the Chronicles, one can sense an air of delight but also a level of seriousness, for the books, after all, address grave issues. Dishonesty, pride, and unrepentance, for instance, are not to be taken lightly. But Lewis offered hope to his readers—hope that someday they, too, may reach Aslan's country. Then those who have chosen the right path will see reality as it truly is, namely something far grander and infinitely more majestic than anything beyond the capacity of our imagination or reason.

In *The Horse and His Boy*, after many trials, the young boy Shasta is lost in a fog. He is exhausted, miserable, and (except for the horse he is riding) alone. Suddenly, he senses something walking beside him. Though he does not know it yet, the presence is Aslan the great lion, the king above all high kings in Narnia and the son of the Emperor-beyond-the-Sea. Shasta is afraid, but the lion calmly tells the boy to share the story of his sorrows.[2]

So Shasta tells of his many adventures and the dangers he has recently faced, including unpleasant encounters with lions. Aslan tells him that he was the lion in all the encounters. It was Aslan who directed Shasta to meet up with Aravis, who comforted him in the form of a cat while Shasta waited alone for his friends, who protected him from jackals, who caused the horses to hurry in order for Shasta to warn Anvard of a surprise attack. And it was Aslan who saved Shasta's life many years earlier by pushing the boat in which the child lay to a shore where a man sat at midnight.[3] At every step of Shasta's life, Aslan was with him, whether he realized it or not. So, too, God is with us every day.

Deep down inside us, as Lewis would say, there is a longing—a desire for joy that eludes us and that nothing on earth can satisfy. Only Christ, "the way and the truth and the life" (John 14:6), can fill the void. Each day, believed Lewis, our actions—however small or great—move us closer to virtue or closer to vice, closer to truth or closer to error, closer to God or further from Him. The moral choices we make build up or tear down our character. And the choices contribute either to the side of good or the side of evil in the battle raging across our world.

May the Golden Rules of Narnia help us move in the right direction and transform our lives so that we may "not be overcome by evil, but overcome evil with good" (Romans 12:21). Like Aslan with Shasta, Christ has been with us and continues to be with us every step of the way. Each day brings those who love Him closer to His kingdom and to the fulfillment of their longing.

Appendix

Chronicles of Narnia Plot Summaries

The following plot summaries of the Chronicles of Narnia are presented in the order in which the books were originally published. Even those familiar with the Chronicles may wish to read these summaries as a refresher. Those unfamiliar with the series must be warned that the summaries reveal key plot points.

The Lion, the Witch and the Wardrobe (1950)

Four English children (Peter, Susan, Edmund, and Lucy) are sent to live in the country in order to avoid the German air attacks of World War II. In the home of Professor Digory Kirke, Lucy finds and hides in a wardrobe, by which she magically enters the land of Narnia and meets Tumnus the faun. After Lucy returns, the other children do not believe her story. Later, though, both Edmund and Lucy enter the wardrobe and reach Narnia. Lucy again meets with Tumnus, while Edmund encounters the White Witch (calling herself the queen of Narnia), who convinces Edmund that it is in his best interests to deliver his brother and sisters to her home.

All four children enter Narnia via the wardrobe and discover that Tumnus is missing. They decide to help the faun but are found by Mr. Beaver, who leads the children to safety and, with Mrs. Beaver, explains the situation. The witch has no rightful claim to call herself queen. Through spells, she has made it always winter in Narnia and never Christmas. The beavers tell the children about a prophecy involving four humans: When they sit on the four thrones in the castle Cair Paravel, there will be peace in Narnia and the dark time of the witch will be over. They also speak to the children about the lion Aslan and rumors of his return to Narnia.

Edmund slips away and betrays his siblings by visiting the witch. The beavers realize the danger and hastily leave their home, taking the children with them, in the hopes of reaching the meeting place where Aslan will arrive. The witch tries to find the children, but her plans are foiled when Narnia begins to thaw and Aslan arrives. She consults with Aslan regarding the life of the traitor Edmund. Their agreement to spare Edmund's life involves the sacrifice of Aslan, who is later resurrected. The witch is killed, her army is defeated, and the four children reign as kings and queens for many years. Finally, they return home via the wardrobe and realize that no time at all has passed in their world and they are once again children.

Prince Caspian (1951)

Peter, Susan, Edmund, and Lucy are at a train station when they are suddenly pulled into Narnia. Arriving at the ruins of a once-great castle, they realize they are in fact in the ruins of the castle

Cair Paravel, where they once lived when they ruled Narnia.

The children witness two soldiers attempting to murder a dwarf. The children rescue the dwarf, and the soldiers flee. The dwarf (Trumpkin) explains that he has been sent by Prince Caspian to seek help that was called for by using a magic horn. The children explain that they must be the help that was summoned, but they have trouble convincing Trumpkin of this.

Trumpkin tells the story of Caspian. Miraz, a Telmarine and Caspian's uncle, has claimed the throne of Narnia through deceit and treachery. Caspian's father was the rightful king, but Miraz murdered him. Caspian was tutored by Doctor Cornelius, a kind old gentleman who is half dwarf. Cornelius told Caspian stories of old Narnia and talking animals. Most of the talking beasts and other Narnian creatures, such as dwarfs, are living in hiding. When the wife of Miraz gave birth to a son, Caspian learned that he must flee or be killed by Miraz.

Caspian met up with two dwarfs (Trumpkin and Nikabrik) and a badger (Trufflehunter). Caspian explained that he is the rightful heir to the throne, and the Narnian beasts gathered to discuss their plans. Miraz, however, had already brought together an army of Telmarines and seeks to wipe out the rebellion led by Caspian.

Peter and Edmund arrive to assist Caspian, while Susan and Lucy meet up with Aslan. Nikabrik has brought a hag and a werewolf to Caspian and tells Caspian they can call up great power by summoning the White Witch. Caspian refuses to use that sort of power. Peter challenges Miraz to single combat in order to decide the victor in the battle. Miraz is goaded by his own men into accepting the challenge and is defeated. The brave talking mouse Reepicheep is introduced, and after his tail is cut off in combat, Aslan heals him. A battle takes place, the Narnians are victorious, and with the approval of Aslan, Caspian claims his rightful place as king of Narnia.

The Voyage of the "Dawn Treader" (1952)

While Peter is being tutored by Professor Kirke, and while Susan is traveling to America with their parents, Edmund and Lucy are sent to stay with their aunt and uncle. Their cousin, Eustace Clarence Scrubb, who enjoys teasing them about their stories of Narnia, is pulled into Narnia while looking at a painting of a ship. Edmund and Lucy are also pulled into Narnia in this manner. They are taken aboard the Narnian ship *Dawn Treader* and are reunited with King Caspian and Reepicheep. They also meet Captain Drinian and other crew members. The crew is searching for seven lost lords of Narnia. Eustace complains and, in general, makes a nuisance of himself (some of his musings are presented in diary form).

The crew members encounter many challenges on their journey, including seeing Caspian and others captured and sold into slavery. Following a storm, they reach another island. Desiring to avoid work, Eustace wanders off, witnesses the death of a dragon, and enters a cave, where he finds treasure and then falls asleep. When he wakes, he realizes he has been transformed into a dragon. After spending some time in this form, Eustace is transformed back into a human by Aslan. Eustace experiences a dramatic change for the better in his character following this experience.

On another island, the adventurers discover a magic pool that transforms anything it touches to gold. Caspian and Edmund begin arguing over the claim to the magic pool, but then Aslan appears and clouds their memory of the pool. They name the place Deathwater Island and leave.

Next, they reach an island inhabited by invisible creatures known as Dufflepuds (or Duffers), who have been made invisible by a magician named Coriakin. Lucy bravely agrees to enter Coriakin's home in the hopes of breaking the spell. After an encounter with Aslan and the magician, Lucy succeeds in freeing the Duffers of their invisibility.

The *Dawn Treader* then travels to the mysterious Dark Island, where the crew members rescue one of the missing Narnian lords. They arrive at another island, where they find the last three missing lords asleep at what appears to be an enchanted banquet table. The adventurers meet a star, Ramandu, and his daughter.

After some convincing, the crew agrees to continue the journey. Edmund, Eustace, Lucy, and Reepicheep travel to the end of the world. Reepicheep continues the journey to Aslan's country alone. The others are met by a lamb, later revealed to be Aslan. The lamb tells them that there is a way into Aslan's country from their own world, but the lion is not known by that name in their world.

The Silver Chair (1953)

Eustace is called back to Narnia with a classmate named Jill Pole. Eustace falls off a cliff but is blown to safety by Aslan. Jill meets Aslan and he explains why the children were called to Narnia. Prince Rilian, son of the now aged King Caspian, is missing and they must find him. Aslan is careful to tell Jill of four signs he will give that they must follow no matter what the consequences.

The first sign—that Eustace must greet the first person in Narnia he recognizes as a friend—is missed, thus making the children's task of finding Prince Rilian more difficult. Nevertheless, with the aid of a marsh-wiggle guide named Puddleglum, Jill and Eustace begin their search for Rilian. They encounter the giants of Harfang and, though they are treated kindly, learn that the giants intend to eat them.

They escape to an underground world populated by beings who serve the queen of Underland. There they meet an enchanted young man who later is revealed to be Prince Rilian. He tells them that the queen of Underland plans to overthrow the world above and make herself queen, with Rilian as king. The children and Puddleglum help Rilian escape but are confronted by the queen, who attempts to confuse them with a spell. Puddleglum refuses to believe her lies and bravely breaks the enchantment. Rilian kills her after she transforms into a serpent and attacks.

The children, Puddleglum, and Rilian escape to the surface in time to be present for the death of King Caspian. Eustace and Jill are called back to Aslan's Mountain, where Caspian is revived by the blood of a lion. Eustace and Jill return to their world and, with the help of Caspian, scare off bullies who had been chasing them just before Aslan called them.

The Horse and His Boy (1954)

This story, which takes place during the reign of Peter, Susan, Edmund, and Lucy over Narnia, revolves around a boy named

Shasta, a young Calormene named Aravis, and two talking Narnian horses (Bree and Hwin). Shasta learns that his father, who treats him poorly, is not really his father after all and that Shasta may in fact be Narnian. With the help of Bree, Shasta escapes in order to avoid being sold into slavery and seeks to return to Narnia. Along the way, the two encounter Aravis, who is also fleeing, but for a different reason (she hopes to avoid an arranged marriage). Aravis is riding a talking Narnian horse named Hwin.

The four join forces in order to reach Narnia. Their plan involves passing through the city of Tashbaan, but during this attempt, Shasta is mistaken for young Prince Corin of Archenland (a friendly neighboring kingdom of Narnia) and is taken in by Susan, Edmund, Tumnus, and other Narnians. Prince Rabadash, a son of the Tisroc (the leader of Calormen), is seeking to marry Queen Susan, but the Narnians rightly fear that if she refuses, Rabadash will take her by force. The real Prince Corin returns and meets Shasta, who departs to meet up again with Aravis, Bree, and Hwin. Meanwhile, the Narnians escape and, as a result, anger Prince Rabadash, who proposes that he be allowed to take a contingent of men on horseback and attack Archenland and then take Narnia in order to capture Susan and take her as his bride.

Prior to meeting up with Shasta and the horses, Aravis overhears the plans of Rabadash. When Aravis is reunited with her friends, they decide to ride as fast as they can to warn Archenland of the surprise attack. An encounter with a lion leaves Aravis injured and Bree and Hwin also unable to continue. They are cared for by the Hermit of the Southern March. Shasta continues with his quest to warn Archenland, which he does.

Anticipating an attack, Archenland defeats Rabadash and his men. During deliberations over the punishment of Rabadash, Aslan appears, and despite many cautions on the part of Aslan, Rabadash continues with his troublesome behavior and is turned into a donkey and sent back to Tashbaan, where he may regain his true form at a public festival. It is revealed that Shasta is really named Cor and is twin brother to Corin. The king of Archenland rejoices at the return of his lost child and heir to the throne.

The Magician's Nephew (1955)

The story takes place many years before the events of *The Lion, the Witch and the Wardrobe* and centers on the child Digory and his friend Polly. Digory's Uncle Andrew tricks Polly into vanishing into an unknown world, and Digory has little choice but to attempt to help her. Both children arrive at the Wood between the Worlds, a sort of in-between place where they discover they can enter other worlds.

They enter Charn and, as a result of Digory's curiosity and bullying of Polly, release the powerful enchantress Jadis (the White Witch). Jadis arrives in London with plans to take over the world, but Digory and Polly manage to return her to the Wood between the Worlds along with Uncle Andrew, a cabby, and a horse.

They all then fall into an empty world and witness the creation of Narnia by Aslan. Certain animals are given the gift of speech and intelligence. After a failed attempt to harm Aslan, Jadis flees. Digory, concerned for the health of his seriously ill mother, asks Aslan for assistance. Riding upon a flying horse, Digory follows the instructions of Aslan and arrives at a garden. He encounters

Jadis and is tempted by her and then takes one apple, as requested by Aslan, to be planted for the protection of Narnia. Because humans have allowed evil to enter Narnia, Aslan charges them to govern the land, appointing the cabby (Frank) and his wife (Helen) to be the first king and queen of Narnia.

Digory, Polly, and Andrew return to London, and Digory's mother is healed after eating the apple provided by Aslan. The seed of the fruit is planted, and we learn that the wood used to build the magical wardrobe in *The Lion, the Witch and the Wardrobe* was taken from the tree that grew from the Narnian fruit.

The Last Battle (1956)

Many years have passed since humans have visited Narnia. An ape named Shift discovers a lion skin and, by manipulating a donkey named Puzzle into wearing a disguise, convinces other Narnians that Puzzle is Aslan. Shift's deceptions soon draw the attention of the neighboring and warlike Calormenes, who, with the help of a Narnian cat named Ginger, begin to manipulate Shift into making various decrees in the name of Aslan.[1]

King Tirian of Narnia and his unicorn friend Jewel hear that Aslan has returned. Their excitement soon turns to concern when they hear that Aslan has ordered trees with living spirits in them to be cut down and find that talking Narnian horses have been ordered to work and are treated harshly by Calormenes. Tirian and Jewel kill two Calormenes and escape but then give themselves up.

Following a brief encounter with Shift, Tirian is separated from Jewel and is tied up. Tirian cries out for help, and Aslan sends Eustace and Jill. They rescue Tirian and together begin to formulate a plan to overthrow Shift and the Calormenes when Jill discovers that Puzzle has only been pretending to be Aslan. They take Puzzle and hope to overthrow Shift and the Calormenes by showing the Narnians that it was all a scheme.

Their plan is preempted and, instead, they fight the last battle and are ultimately thrown into a stable that leads to Aslan's country. Aslan brings an end to Narnia, and those faithful to him enter his country, where they are reunited with loved ones, including many characters from the Chronicles, such as Reepicheep, Tumnus, and others.

Notes

Introduction

1. The ages of human characters in the Chronicles of Narnia are based on Lewis's "Outline of Narnian History So Far As It Is Known," in Walter Hooper, *C. S. Lewis: A Companion and Guide* (New York: HarperCollins, 1996), 420–423. Ages of the characters (also based on Lewis's chronology) are also found in Paul F. Ford, *Companion to Narnia*, 4th ed. (San Francisco: HarperSanFrancisco, 1994), appendix 2, which in turn is based on material in Walter Hooper, *Past Watchful Dragons* (New York: Macmillan, 1979), 41–44.
2. C. S. Lewis, *An Experiment in Criticism* (New York: Cambridge University Press, 1961), 70.
3. Walter Hooper, "Narnia: The Author, the Critics, and the Tale," in *The Longing for a Form: Essays on the Fiction of C. S. Lewis,* ed. Peter J. Schakel (Kent, OH: Kent State University Press, 1977), 105.
4. Lewis, *Experiment in Criticism*, especially chapter 3.
5. Jim Ware, *God of the Fairy Tale: Finding Truth in the Land of Make-Believe* (Colorado Springs, CO: Shaw, 2003), 7.
6. Ware, 7.
7. C. S. Lewis, "On Three Ways of Writing for Children," in *Of Other Worlds: Essays and Stories*, ed. Walter Hooper (New York: Harcourt Brace, 1966), 31.

CHAPTER 1

1. C. S. Lewis, *The Last Battle* (New York: Harper Trophy, 2000), 3. Unless otherwise specified, editions of the Chronicles cited are the paperback Harper Trophy editions published in 2000.
2. C. S. Lewis, *Mere Christianity* (New York: Macmillan, 1960), 45.
3. Paul F. Ford, *Companion to Narnia*, 4th ed. (San Francisco: HarperSanFrancisco, 1994), under "right and wrong."
4. Alan Jacobs, "The Second Coming of C. S. Lewis," First Things, http://www.firstthings.com/ftissues/ft9411/jacobs.html, accessed February 26, 2005.
5. In addition to Lewis's own works, for some helpful resources on Lewis's ethics, see Gilbert Meilaender, *The Taste for the Other: The Social and Ethical Thought of C. S. Lewis* (Grand Rapids, MI: Eerdmans, 1998); John Randolph Willis, *Pleasures Forevermore: The Theology of C. S. Lewis* (Chicago: Loyola University Press, 1983); John A. Sims, *Missionaries to the Skeptics: Christian Apologists for the Twentieth Century: C. S. Lewis, E. J. Carnell, and Reinhold Niebuhr* (Macon, GA: Mercer University Press, 1995); Will Vaus, *Mere Theology: A Guide to the Thought of C. S. Lewis* (Downers Grove, IL: InterVarsity, 2004); and Armand M. Nicholi, *The Question of God: C. S. Lewis and Sigmund Freud Debate God, Love, Sex, and the Meaning of Life* (New York: Free Press, 2002).
6. C. S. Lewis, *Surprised by Joy: The Shape of My Early Life* (New York: Harcourt Brace, 1956), 178–180, 190–191. Also see David C. Downing, *The Most Reluctant Convert* (Downers Grove, IL: InterVarsity, 2002).
7. Nicholi, 59.
8. Meilaender, 235.

9. C. S. Lewis, *Rehabilitations and Other Essays* (London: Oxford University Press, 1939), 64, cited in Wayne Martindale and Jerry Root, eds., *The Quotable Lewis* (Wheaton, IL: Tyndale, 1989), 474.
10. C. S. Lewis, *Till We Have Faces: A Myth Retold* (New York: Harcourt, 1956), 305.
11. Lewis, *Last Battle*, 195.
12. Meilaender, 235.
13. C. S. Lewis, *The Four Loves* (New York: Harcourt Brace, 1960), 120.
14. C. S. Lewis, letter dated September 12, 1933, in *They Stand Together: The Letters of C. S. Lewis to Arthur Greeves, 1914–1963*, ed. Walter Hooper (London: Collins, 1979), 465, cited in Martindale and Root, 265.
15. Lewis, *Mere Christianity*, 82–83.
16. Cited in William Dyrness, *Christian Apologetics in a World Community* (Downers Grove, IL: InterVarsity, 1983), 153. The quote is actually Lactantius (c. 240–320) quoting Epicurus.
17. C. S. Lewis, *The Problem of Pain* (New York: Macmillan, 1962).
18. C. S. Lewis, *A Grief Observed* (New York, Bantam Books, 1976).
19. C. S. Lewis, *The Magician's Nephew* (New York: Harper Trophy, 2000), 130, 146, 148, 151.
20. Lewis, *Mere Christianity*, 117.
21. Lewis, *Mere Christianity*, 86.
22. Lewis, *Mere Christianity*, 77.
23. Lewis, *Magician's Nephew*, 153.
24. Lewis, *Magician's Nephew*, 171.
25. Lewis, *Magician's Nephew*, 176.

CHAPTER 2

1. C. S. Lewis, *The Voyage of the "Dawn Treader"* (New York: Harper Trophy, 2000), 117, 120.
2. The ancient Greeks listed justice, prudence, temperance, and fortitude (courage) as the cardinal virtues. The early Christians added the virtues of faith, hope, and love.
3. C. S. Lewis, *Mere Christianity* (New York: Macmillan, 1952), 76.
4. C. S. Lewis, *The Screwtape Letters*, rev. ed. (New York: Macmillan, 1982), 135.
5. Lewis, *Screwtape Letters*, 136–137, 139.
6. Eustace whispers to Jill that the marsh-wiggle has both "pluck" and "cheek" (C. S. Lewis, *The Silver Chair* [New York: Harper Trophy, 2000], 105).
7. Lewis, *Silver Chair,* 167.
8. This sequence with the queen depicts the Neoplatonism present in *The Silver Chair* and also provides insights into the intellectual struggles of empiricism and the nature of reality. See Thomas C. Peters, *Simply C. S. Lewis: A Beginner's Guide to His Life and Works* (Wheaton, IL: Crossway, 1997), 95–97; and Paul F. Ford, *Companion to Narnia*, 4th ed. (San Francisco: HarperSanFrancisco, 1994), under "Plato."
9. Lewis, *Silver Chair,* 180.
10. Lewis, *Silver Chair,* 232.
11. C. S. Lewis, *The Horse and His Boy* (New York: Harper Trophy, 2000), 7–10, 145, 154, chapters 6, 13.
12. Lewis, *Horse and His Boy*, 143–144.
13. For a helpful discussion of Reepicheep's courage, see Kathryn Lindskoog, *Journey into Narnia* (Pasadena, CA: Hope, 1998), 63–65.

14. C. S. Lewis, *Prince Caspian* (New York: Harper Trophy, 2000), 206–210.
15. Lewis, *Voyage of the "Dawn Treader,"* 136–138, 177–179, 244.
16. Female and male characters are often stereotyped in the Chronicles. However, as Paul Ford observes, "Although the books are filled with superficially sexist references, Lewis's insights into character often reveal a basic sympathy for the equality of women" (Ford, under "Sexism").
17. Though not explicitly noted, Helen, the wife of the cabby Frank in *The Magician's Nephew*, also exhibits courage by her willingness to leave all that is familiar behind her in order to rule Narnia with her husband (C. S. Lewis, *The Magician's Nephew* [New York: Harper Trophy, 2000], 149–150, 187).
18. Lewis, *Horse and His Boy*, chapter 3; Lewis, *Silver Chair*, 142–143; Lewis, *Magician's Nephew*, 39–41.
19. C. S. Lewis, *The Lion, the Witch and the Wardrobe* (New York: Harper Trophy, 2000), 184; Lewis, *Horse and His Boy*, 176, 179, 182, and so on; Lewis, *The Lion, the Witch and the Wardrobe*, 59; Lewis, *Prince Caspian*, 147; Lewis, *Voyage of the "Dawn Treader,"* 97–98, 142–143, 146–147.
20. Lewis, *Voyage of the "Dawn Treader,"* 141–142.
21. Lewis, *Voyage of the "Dawn Treader,"* 207–208, 212.
22. Lewis, *Voyage of the "Dawn Treader,"* 215–216.
23. Lewis, *Voyage of the "Dawn Treader,"* 217.
24. Lewis, *Voyage of the "Dawn Treader,"* 216–217.
25. Lewis, *Magician's Nephew*, 25. For Lewis's insights on the connections between the materialist and magic, see Lewis's 1941 preface to *The Screwtape Letters*; C. S. Lewis, *English Literature*

in the Sixteenth Century Excluding Drama (New York: Oxford University Press, 1973), 13–14; and especially C. S. Lewis, *The Abolition of Man* (New York: Macmillan, 1955), 83, 87–89.

26. Lewis, *Magician's Nephew*, 17–18, 24–26.
27. Lewis, *Magician's Nephew*, 75–76, 82–83.
28. Lewis, *Magician's Nephew*, 105–106, 110–118, 136–139.
29. Lewis, *Magician's Nephew*, 202. It is unclear, however, if Andrew's experience resulted in true repentance.
30. J. P. Moreland, *Love Your God with All Your Mind: The Role of Reason in the Life of the Soul* (Colorado Springs, CO: NavPress, 1997), 110.
31. Lewis, *Voyage of the "Dawn Treader,"* 213. A coracle is a small boat.

CHAPTER 3

1. C. S. Lewis, *The Voyage of the "Dawn Treader"* (New York: Harper Trophy, 2000), 62, 74; C. S. Lewis, *The Silver Chair* (New York: Harper Trophy, 2000), 5; C. S. Lewis, *The Horse and His Boy* (New York: Harper Trophy, 2000), 43; C. S. Lewis, *The Magician's Nephew* (New York: Harper Trophy, 2000), 102; C. S. Lewis, *The Last Battle* (New York: Harper Trophy, 2000), 4, 10.
2. C. S. Lewis, *Mere Christianity* (New York: Macmillan, 1952), 17–18.
3. C. S. Lewis, *Miracles* (New York: Macmillan, 1978), 37.
4. The terms "fairness" and "justice" will be used interchangeably throughout this chapter, as will the terms "unfairness" and "injustice."
5. Stanley J. Grenz and Jay T. Smith, *Pocket Dictionary of Ethics* (Downers Grove, IL: InterVarsity, 2003), under "justice."

6. Lewis, *Mere Christianity,* 76.
7. *The Compact Oxford English Dictionary,* 2nd edition (Oxford: Oxford University Press, 1991), under "injustice."
8. Lewis, *Mere Christianity,* 46.
9. C. S. Lewis, *The Lion, the Witch and the Wardrobe* (New York: Harper Trophy, 2000), 79.
10. Lewis, *The Lion, the Witch and the Wardrobe,* 142.
11. American editions prior to 1994 substitute "the trunk of the World Ash Tree" for the Secret Hill. If the traditional interpretation of the Emperor-beyond-the-Sea representing God the Father and Aslan being a Christ figure (the Son) is followed, then the fact that the Deep Magic is written in three places may hint at the Trinity. The Deep Magic is written on the scepter of the Father and also on the Stone Table where the Son will be sacrificed; the reference to the fire-stones of the Secret Hill, then, may in some way refer to the Holy Spirit (compare Acts 2:3; 1 Thessalonians 5:19). Paul Ford, however, disagrees, as he stated, "No biblical allusion is intended" (Paul F. Ford, *Companion to Narnia,* 4th ed. [San Francisco: HarperSanFrancisco, 1994], under "Secret Hill"). Ford cites Professor Thomas W. Craik, who suggests that the image of the Secret Hill is "suggestive and not precise." Indeed, Craik considers the image suggestive in a sinister sense, "with a hint of (human?) sacrifice." At any rate, there are clearer examples of representation of the Trinity in the Chronicles, such as on page 165 in *The Horse and His Boy,* where Aslan, in answer to a question about who he is, responds in trinitarian manner with the word "Myself."

12. Lewis, *The Lion, the Witch and the Wardrobe,* 142.
13. Lewis, *The Lion, the Witch and the Wardrobe,* 163.
14. Lewis, *Voyage of the "Dawn Treader,"* 111.
15. Lewis, *Mere Christianity,* 17.
16. Lewis, *Silver Chair,* 241–242.
17. C. S. Lewis, *Prince Caspian* (New York: Harper Trophy, 2000), 10.
18. Lewis, *Prince Caspian,* 125, 128.
19. Lewis, *Last Battle,* 21.
20. Lewis, *Last Battle,* 22.
21. Lewis, *Last Battle,* 31.
22. Ford, under "Gumpas."
23. Lewis, *Voyage of the "Dawn Treader,"* 58–59.
24. Lewis, *Voyage of the "Dawn Treader,"* 62.
25. Lewis has been criticized for promoting racism in the Chronicles by his depiction of the Calormenes as a dark-skinned, garlic-breathed, turban-wearing race. Paul Ford wrote, "Like many Englishmen of his era, Lewis was unconsciously unsympathetic to things and people Middle-Eastern. That Lewis opts into this cultural blindness is regrettable" (Ford, under "Calormen"). However, the manner in which the Calormenes are depicted may have more to do with the style Lewis chose for the Narnia books (fairy tales with strong elements of Romance literature) than with any racial prejudice. It is true that in *The Last Battle* the renegade dwarfs taunt the Calormene soldiers by referring to their dark skin, but these are bad dwarfs and their behavior is not typical of the courtesy and civility of Narnia (Lewis, *Last Battle,* 144). Peter Schakel observes that the Calormenes "are Moors: they are identified

by their dress, weapons, and manners as the traditional enemy in medieval romances. More important, however, than Lewis's use of this convention are his frequent departures from and adaptations of it. The enemies in most of the books are not dark. . . . Even more significantly, not all Calormenes are evil—a notable exception is Emeth . . . and one even becomes queen of Archenland [Aravis], when she marries the fair-skinned hero of *The Horse and His Boy*" (Peter J. Schakel, *Reading with the Heart: The Way into Narnia* [Grand Rapids, MI: Eerdmans, 1979], 12–13).

26. Lewis, *Horse and His Boy,* 51; Lewis, *Last Battle,* 207.
27. Lewis, *Horse and His Boy,* 56.
28. Ford, under "Calormen."
29. Lewis, *Horse and His Boy,* 121.
30. Lewis, *Last Battle,* 4.
31. Lewis, *Last Battle,* 9.
32. Lewis, *Last Battle,* 10.
33. Lewis, *Mere Christianity,* 18.
34. For the phrase "deep down inside," see Lewis, *The Lion, the Witch and the Wardrobe,* 89; *Prince Caspian,* 152; *Voyage of the "Dawn Treader,"* 4; *Silver Chair,* 101; *Magician's Nephew,* 195; and *Last Battle,* 97.
35. Athanasius argued against the popular Arian heresy, which taught that Jesus was a created being and consequently was not divine.
36. Scripture, too, highlights the integrated nature of virtues. Micah 6:8, for instance, reads, "What does the LORD require of you? To act justly and to love mercy and to walk humbly with your God."

CHAPTER 4

1. C. S. Lewis, *The Last Battle* (New York: Harper Trophy, 2000), 14.
2. Walter Elwell, ed., *Evangelical Dictionary of Theology* (Grand Rapids, MI: Baker, 1984), under "Honesty."
3. Stanley J. Grenz and Jay T. Smith, *Pocket Dictionary of Ethics* (Downers Grove, IL: InterVarsity, 2003), under "honesty."
4. See, for example, Dallas Willard, "Truth in the Fire: C. S. Lewis and Pursuit of Truth Today," http://www.dwillard.org/articles/artview.asp?artID=68, accessed February 24, 2005. Also see the section on C. S. Lewis in Gordon Lewis, *Testing Christianity's Truth Claims: Approaches to Christian Apologetics* (New York: University Press of America, 1990), 331–339.
5. C. S. Lewis, *An Experiment in Criticism* (New York: Cambridge University Press, 1961), 56, 67.
6. Lewis, *Experiment in Criticism*, 67–68.
7. *The Compact Oxford English Dictionary*, 2nd edition (Oxford: Oxford University Press, 1991), under "dishonesty," "probity."
8. C. S. Lewis, *The Lion, the Witch and the Wardrobe* (New York: Harper Trophy, 2000), 89.
9. Elwell, under "honesty."
10. Gleason Archer, *Encyclopedia of Bible Difficulties* (Grand Rapids, MI: Zondervan, 1982), 155.
11. For a brief but helpful overview of ethical conflicts such as these, see Scott B. Rae, *Moral Choices*, 2nd ed. (Grand Rapids, MI: Zondervan, 2000), 34–35.
12. Lewis, *The Lion, the Witch and the Wardrobe*, 25–26.

13. In a similar incident, Lucy is honest in *Prince Caspian* when it comes to saying that she has seen Aslan. This time Edmund is open to believing her, showing that he has made progress in his character growth. C. S. Lewis, *Prince Caspian* (New York: Harper Trophy, 2000), 125–128.
14. Lewis, *Voyage of the "Dawn Treader,"* 15–16. Lucy, however, does give in to her urge later and hugs Reepicheep as he is preparing to enter Aslan's country (244).
15. Lewis, *The Lion, the Witch and the Wardrobe,* 114–116.
16. Cornelius embodies a number of characteristics Lewis admired in educators, including the importance of valuing truth.
17. Lewis, *Prince Caspian,* 51.
18. C. S. Lewis, *The Silver Chair* (New York: Harper Trophy, 2000), 89.
19. Lewis, *Silver Chair*, 131.
20. Lewis, *Silver Chair*, 61. See also 226.
21. Lewis, *Silver Chair*, 227.
22. C. S. Lewis, *The Horse and His Boy* (New York: Harper Trophy, 2000), 214.
23. Paul F. Ford, *Companion to Narnia*, 4th ed. (San Francisco: HarperSanFrancisco, 1994), under "Shift."
24. In two of Aesop's fables a donkey wears a lion's skin for purposes of deception (*Aesop's Fables,* trans. S. A. Handford [New York: Puffin, 1964], fables 108 and 109). This is just one instance of numerous literary allusions found in the Chronicles. More detailed accounts of such allusions are included in Ford's *Companion to Narnia*, under "Biblical Allusions" and "Literary Allusions."

25. C. S. Lewis, *Last Battle*, 32. Later the ape is overt in his deception, blatantly lying and claiming to be a man (35).
26. Lewis, *Last Battle*, 37.
27. Lewis, *Last Battle*, 38–39.
28. Lewis, *Last Battle*, 131, 163–164.
29. Lewis, *Horse and His Boy*, 71–73.
30. Lewis, *Last Battle*, 62–64.
31. In chapter 6 of *Reading with the Heart: The Way into Narnia* (Grand Rapids, MI: Eerdmans, 1979), Peter Schakel comments on the many disguises of Aravis, suggesting Lewis may be using this as a literary device to indicate her confusion of identity.
32. See, for example, Lewis, *Last Battle*, 188–189, where Aslan clearly opposes the deception that Aslan and Tash are the same.
33. Lewis, *Last Battle*, 84–85.
34. Douglas Groothuis, "Why Truth Matters Most: An Apologetic for Truth-Seeking in Postmodern Times," *Journal of the Evangelical Theological Society* 47, no. 3 (September 2004): 453.

CHAPTER 5

1. C. S. Lewis, *The Lion, the Witch and the Wardrobe* (New York: Harper Trophy, 2000), 151–155.
2. C. S. Lewis, *The Magician's Nephew* (New York: Harper Trophy, 2000), 73.
3. Stephen Liggins, "According to the Son," http://cslewis.drzeus.net/papers/son.html, accessed February 22, 2005. This article comes from the spring 1998 issue of *Southern Cross Quarterly*.
4. *The Compact Oxford English Dictionary*, 2nd ed. (Oxford: Oxford University Press, 1991), under "mercy."

5. See, for instance, C. S. Lewis, "On Forgiveness," in *The Weight of Glory and Other Addresses*, rev. ed. (New York: Macmillan, 1980), 125.
6. See, for instance, W. H. Lewis and Walter Hooper, eds., *Letters of C. S. Lewis*, rev. ed. (New York: Harcourt, 1993), 418, letter dated January 31, 1952; C. S. Lewis, "The Humanitarian Theory of Punishment," in *God in the Dock: Essays on Theology and Ethics,* ed. Walter Hooper (Grand Rapids, MI: Eerdmans, 1970), 294.
7. *Compact Oxford English Dictionary*, under "cruelty."
8. C. S. Lewis, *Mere Christianity* (New York: Macmillan, 1952), 49.
9. Leland Ryken, James C. Wilhoit, Tremper Longman III, eds., *Dictionary of Biblical Imagery* (Downers Grove, IL: InterVarsity, 1998), under "mercy."
10. Joel B. Green and Scot McKnight, eds., *Dictionary of Jesus and the Gospels* (Downers Grove, IL: InterVarsity, 1992), under "mercy."
11. T. Desmond Alexander and Brian S. Rosner, eds., *New Dictionary of Biblical Theology* (Downers Grove, IL: InterVarsity, 2000), under "mercy."
12. For a more detailed analysis of Pascal's anthropological argument, see my article "Greatness and Wretchedness: The Usefulness of Pascal's Anthropological Argument in Apologetics," *Christian Research Journal* 27, no. 2 (2004): 31–40.
13. "Cruel" is used in Job 30:21 in translations such as the NASB and KJV, while the NIV uses "ruthless."
14. J. D. Douglas, N. Hillyer, D. R. W. Wood, and others, *New Bible Dictionary*, 3rd ed. (Leicester, England: InterVarsity, 1996), under "wicked."
15. Lewis, *The Lion, the Witch and the Wardrobe,* 179; C. S. Lewis, *The Horse and His Boy* (New York: Harper Trophy, 2000), 214; C. S. Lewis,

The Last Battle (New York: Harper Trophy, 2000), 164–167.

16. Her obvious goal is to circumvent the prophecy that four humans would result in her downfall. A secondary goal involves the elimination of Aslan. A third goal involves the reclaiming of Narnia and subsequent punishment of those who opposed her.
17. See Lewis, *The Lion, the Witch and the Wardrobe,* chapters 13 and 14.
18. Lewis, *Horse and His Boy,* 213, 215.
19. Lewis, *Horse and His Boy,* 216.
20. Lewis, *Horse and His Boy,* 209.
21. Lewis, *Horse and His Boy,* 211.
22. Lewis, *Horse and His Boy,* 219.
23. Lewis, *Last Battle,* 175–176. Talking creatures who move to Aslan's left are transformed into regular animals.
24. She had pulled the iron bar off a lamppost in England. Lewis, *Magician's Nephew,* 116.
25. She is not human but, according to Mr. Beaver, would like others to think so. See *The Lion, the Witch and the Wardrobe,* 81. In *The Magician's Nephew* we learn that Jadis came from another world. Consequently, it is unclear whether Mr. Beaver's other comments about her are true. For instance, he claims Jadis is the daughter of Adam and Lilith.
26. Lewis, *The Lion, the Witch and the Wardrobe,* 134–136.
27. Lewis, *The Lion, the Witch and the Wardrobe,* 34, 111, 116–117.
28. Lewis, *Magician's Nephew,* 87.
29. Lewis, *The Lion, the Witch and the Wardrobe,* 116.
30. Lewis, *The Lion, the Witch and the Wardrobe,* 96.
31. Lewis, *The Lion, the Witch and the Wardrobe,* 113. While the British editions list the name as Maugrim, American editions give

the name as Fenris Ulf. For more on the name change, see Paul F. Ford, *Companion to Narnia*, 4th ed. (San Francisco: HarperSanFrancisco, 1994), under "Fenris Ulf," note 1.

32. Lewis, *Magician's Nephew*, 93.
33. Lewis, *The Lion, the Witch and the Wardrobe*, 31, 113, 118, 119.
34. Lewis, *Magician's Nephew*, 61.
35. Lewis, *Magician's Nephew*, 65.
36. Lewis, *Magician's Nephew*, 69.
37. Lewis, *Magician's Nephew*, 68.
38. Lewis, *Magician's Nephew*, 21. The Witch and Andrew are examples of people who have removed themselves from the moral standard of what Lewis calls the Tao, which in the end will result in their abolition. For more on this, see chapter 4 of *The Abolition of Man*.
39. Lewis, *The Lion, the Witch and the Wardrobe*, 26.
40. Lewis, *The Lion, the Witch and the Wardrobe*, 46.
41. Lewis, *The Lion, the Witch and the Wardrobe*, 44.
42. Lewis, *The Lion, the Witch and the Wardrobe*, 45.
43. Lewis, *The Lion, the Witch and the Wardrobe*, 56.
44. Ford, under "Edmund Pevensie."
45. C. S. Lewis, *The Voyage of the "Dawn Treader"* (New York: Harper Trophy, 2000), 3–4.
46. Lewis, *Voyage of the "Dawn Treader,"* 7–8.
47. Lewis, *Voyage of the "Dawn Treader,"* 27.
48. Lewis, *Voyage of the "Dawn Treader,"* 26, 32, 35.
49. Lewis, *Magician's Nephew*, 24.
50. Lewis, *Magician's Nephew*, 110, 118.

51. C. S. Lewis, "Vivisection," in *God in the Dock* (Grand Rapids, MI: Eerdmans, 1970), 228.
52. Lewis, "The Pains of Animals, A Problem in Theology," in *God in the Dock*, 166–171.
53. C. S. Lewis, *That Hideous Strength* (New York: Macmillan, 1965), 102.
54. C. S. Lewis, *The Problem of Pain* (New York: Macmillan, 1962), 130–131.
55. Lewis, *Problem of Pain*, 138.
56. Lewis, *The Lion, the Witch and the Wardrobe*, 89.
57. Lewis, *Mere Christianity*, 34.
58. J. P. Moreland, Kai Nielsen, and others, *Does God Exist? The Great Debate* (Nashville: Nelson, 1990), 207. The chapter by Dallas Willard, "Language, Being, God, and the Three Stages of Theistic Evidence," is available online at http://www.dwillard.org/articles/artview.asp?artID=42.

CHAPTER 6

1. C. S. Lewis, *The Magician's Nephew* (New York: Harper Trophy, 2000), 193.
2. Lewis, *Magician's Nephew*, 66–67.
3. Lewis, *Magician's Nephew*, 194.
4. Lewis, "Is Progress Possible?" in *God in the Dock: Essays on Theology and Ethics*, ed. Walter Hooper (Grand Rapids, MI: Eerdmans, 1970), 312.

5. C. S. Lewis, "On Living in an Atomic Age," in *Present Concerns,* ed. Walter Hooper (New York: Harcourt, 1986), 73. See also C. S. Lewis, "The World's Last Night," in *The World's Last Night and Other Essays* (New York: Harcourt Brace Jovanovich, 1960).
6. C. S. Lewis, *Mere Christianity* (New York: Macmillan, 1952), 54.
7. See C. S. Lewis, "Why I Am Not a Pacifist," in *The Weight of Glory and Other Addresses,* rev. ed., ed. Walter Hooper (New York: Macmillan, 1980).
8. W. H. Lewis and Walter Hooper, eds., *Letters of C. S. Lewis,* rev. ed. (New York: Harcourt, 1993), 320, letter dated May 8, 1939.
9. See Lewis, "Learning in War-Time," in *Weight of Glory*.
10. C. S. Lewis, *The Screwtape Letters,* rev. ed. (New York: Macmillan, 1982), 27, letter V.
11. C. S. Lewis, "The Conditions for a Just War," in *God in the Dock,* 326.
12. For a Christian introduction to the topic, see Scott B. Rae, *Moral Choices: An Introduction to Ethics,* 2nd ed. (Grand Rapids, MI: Zondervan, 2000), chapter 12; and Robert G. Clouse, *War: Four Christian Views* (Downers Grove, IL: InterVarsity, 1991).
13. Leland Ryken, James C. Wilhoit, and Tremper Longman III, eds., *Dictionary of Biblical Imagery* (Downers Grove, IL: InterVarsity, 1998), under "divine warrior."
14. Rae, 245–246. For a discussion of some of the extreme measures ordered by God and taken by the Israelites in certain instances of warfare, see Gleason L. Archer, *Encyclopedia of Bible Difficulties* (Grand Rapids, MI: Zondervan, 1982); and Lee Strobel, *The Case for Faith* (Grand Rapids, MI: Zondervan, 2000), objection 4.

15. There are notable exceptions, such as Matthew 10:34, where Christ says, "Do not suppose that I have come to bring peace to the earth. I did not come to bring peace, but a sword." Such passages, however, must be interpreted in context.
16. Stanley J. Grenz and Jay T. Smith, *Pocket Dictionary of Ethics* (Downers Grove, IL: InterVarsity, 2003), under "just war theory."
17. C. S. Lewis, *The Last Battle* (New York: Harper Trophy, 2000), 99.
18. Lewis, *Last Battle*, 100. When Jill hears this, she is eager to return to such times and expresses her hope that Narnia will go on forever. Jewel replies that only Aslan's country is eternal, while all other worlds must end, thus foreshadowing the end of Narnia (100–101, 171–182).
19. Although the Golden Age of Narnia lasted but fifteen years in Lewis's later chronology, the years were apparently the apex of peace and prosperity for Narnia.
20. C. S. Lewis, *The Lion, the Witch and the Wardrobe* (New York: Harper Trophy, 2000), 183.
21. Lewis, *The Lion, the Witch and the Wardrobe*, 183. Lewis also offers a hint of environmentalism during the Golden Age when he points out that the kings and queens also protected trees from being felled unnecessarily.
22. C. S. Lewis, *The Horse and His Boy* (New York: Harper Trophy, 2000), 170–171.
23. C. S. Lewis, *Prince Caspian* (New York: Harper Trophy, 2000), 154, 220; Lewis, *The Lion, the Witch and the Wardrobe,* 129, 177.
24. Lewis, *Prince Caspian,* 154–155.

25. Lewis, *The Voyage of the "Dawn Treader"* (New York: Harper Trophy, 2000), 244.
26. Lewis, *The Lion, the Witch and the Wardrobe,* 183; Lewis, *Horse and His Boy,* 114, 171; Lewis, *Voyage of the "Dawn Treader,"* 20; Lewis, *The Silver Chair* (New York: Harper Trophy, 2000), 74.
27. Lewis, *The Lion, the Witch and the Wardrobe,* 108.
28. Lewis, *The Lion, the Witch and the Wardrobe,* 145–147.
29. Lewis, *The Lion, the Witch and the Wardrobe,* 130–133. Whether Lewis intended a literary allusion to "Peter and the Wolf" in this instance is unclear, but it is possible.
30. Lewis, *The Lion, the Witch and the Wardrobe,* chapter 16. Some of those rescued who were once statues were no doubt killed in the ensuing battle against the White Witch. From a worldly perspective, their deaths might seem unfair, but Lewis held to an eternal perspective. What really matters is our eternal destination.
31. Lewis, *The Lion, the Witch and the Wardrobe,* 177.
32. Lewis, *Silver Chair,* 191.
33. A case can be made that perhaps the Narnians go too far in their eradication of the witch's forces even after the defeat of her army, since they pursue her remaining forces with the intent of eliminating them. However, apparently the witch's remaining forces, though greatly weakened and scattered, continue to perform acts of evil. Therefore, the Narnians may be justified in pursing these remaining hostile forces with the intent of destroying them for the greater purposes of peace.
34. Lewis, *Last Battle,* 205.
35. Lewis, *Prince Caspian,* 39.

36. Lewis mentions similar combat situations in at least two of his other fictional works: *Perelandra,* where Ransom must fight the Unman, and *Till We Have Faces,* where Orual fights Argan. Biblically, this type of combat is found in the account of David and Goliath (1 Samuel 17:8-9,32-51).
37. Lewis, *Prince Caspian,* 197–199, 206.
38. Lewis, *Prince Caspian,* 213–215.
39. Lewis, *Horse and His Boy,* 160.
40. Lewis, *Silver Chair,* 191.
41. While there is room for variation in dedicated times of prayer, Lewis considered the time before going to bed the worst time for prayer because one's mind is weary, filled with the events of the day, and prone to wander.
42. C. S. Lewis, *Reflections on the Psalms* (New York: Harcourt, 1958).
43. On managing hectic lives, see Richard Swenson, *Margin: Restoring Emotional, Physical, Financial, and Time Reserves to Overloaded Lives* (Colorado Springs, CO: NavPress, 1995).

Chapter 7

1. C. S. Lewis, *Prince Caspian* (New York: Harper Trophy, 2000), 206.
2. C. S. Lewis, *Mere Christianity* (New York: Macmillan, 1952), 114.
3. Paul F. Ford, *Companion to Narnia,* 4th ed. (San Francisco: HarperSanFrancisco, 1994), under "Obedience."
4. *The Compact Oxford English Dictionary,* 2nd edition (Oxford: Oxford University Press, 1991), under "pride."
5. Lewis, *Mere Christianity,* 109.
6. Lewis, *Mere Christianity,* 110, 112.

7. Lewis, *Mere Christianity*, 113–114.
8. Leland Ryken, James C. Wilhoit, and Tremper Longman III, eds., *Dictionary of Biblical Imagery* (Downers Grove, IL: InterVarsity, 1998), under "humility."
9. Ralph P. Martin and Peter H. Davids, eds., *Dictionary of the Later New Testament and Its Developments* (Downers Grove, IL: InterVarsity, 1997), under "Pride and Humility."
10. Ryken, Wilhoit, and Longman, *Dictionary of Biblical Imagery*, under "pride."
11. Lewis's approach was more along the lines of exploring the question of what God might do in another world to redeem the lost. As a result, Aslan has some interesting parallels to Christ as well as some significant differences or "gaps" in his background. Aslan is the Son of the great Emperor-beyond-the-Sea just as in a similar sense Christ is the Son of God, but details regarding any possible incarnation of Aslan in a sense that parallels that of Christ's incarnation are not provided.
12. C. S. Lewis, *The Lion, the Witch and the Wardrobe* (New York: Harper Trophy, 2000), 141–155.
13. C. S. Lewis, *The Silver Chair* (New York: Harper Trophy, 2000), 237–240.
14. Lewis, *Prince Caspian*, 209–210.
15. C. S. Lewis, "The Efficacy of Prayer," in *The World's Last Night and Other Essays* (New York: Harcourt Brace Jovanovich, 1973), 3–11.
16. Blaise Pascal, *Pensées*, trans. A. J. Krailsheimer (New York: Penguin, 1995), fragment 930/513, 296. Lewis quoted this passage on page 9 of "The Efficacy of Prayer." In *Mere Theology: A Guide to the Thought of C. S. Lewis* (Downers Grove, IL:

InterVarsity, 2004), Will Vaus observed that Lewis's mind on this matter may have changed later in his life. See chapter 20 on "Prayer" in Vaus's book. Also see C. S. Lewis, *Letters to Malcolm: Chiefly on Prayer* (New York: Harcourt, 1964), 51–56, letter X.

17. Lewis, *World's Last Night,* 9.
18. C. S. Lewis, *The Horse and His Boy* (New York: Harper Trophy, 2000), 136.
19. Lewis, *Horse and His Boy,* 46, 48.
20. Lewis, *Horse and His Boy,* 3.
21. Lewis, *Horse and His Boy,* 54.
22. Lewis, *Horse and His Boy,* 212.
23. Lewis, *Horse and His Boy,* 205.
24. The prophecy refers to the saving of Anvard at a time when it would face its greatest danger.
25. Lewis, *Horse and His Boy,* 208.
26. Lewis, *Horse and His Boy,* 204.
27. Lewis, *Prince Caspian,* 208.
28. C. S. Lewis, *The Magician's Nephew* (New York: Harper Trophy, 2000), 174.
29. C. S. Lewis, *The Silver Chair* (New York: Harper Trophy, 2000), 24.
30. C. S. Lewis, *The Last Battle* (New York: Harper Trophy, 2000), 64–65.
31. Lewis, *Horse and His Boy,* 30–32.
32. Lewis, *Horse and His Boy,* 103. This turns out to be false, since by the end of the story Aravis becomes queen of Archenland.
33. Lewis, *Horse and His Boy,* 39–40, 201–202.

34. Lewis, *Horse and His Boy,* 53–54.
35. Lewis, *Horse and His Boy,* 77, 85.
36. Lewis, *Horse and His Boy,* 103.
37. Lewis, *Horse and His Boy,* 151.
38. Lewis, *Horse and His Boy,* 204–205.
39. Lewis, *Horse and His Boy,* 18. His full name is Breehy-hinny-brinny-hoohy-hah.
40. The phrase "Narnia and the North" is mentioned ten times in *The Horse and His Boy*. Aside from three exceptions noted parenthetically, it is uttered by Bree in the other seven instances. See 18, 23, 24, 52, 72 (uttered by a dwarf), 77 (uttered by Tumnus), 87 (mentioned in reference to the direction in which Aslan, in the form of a cat, is facing), 104, 127, and 210. On page 14, Shasta notes that he, too, longs to go north. Lewis also longed for things northern. One of the working titles for *The Horse and His Boy* was *Narnia and the North*.
41. Lewis, *Horse and His Boy,* 13, 16, 17, 23, 44.
42. Lewis, *Horse and His Boy,* 22, 48.
43. Lewis, *Horse and His Boy,* 53.
44. Lewis, *Horse and His Boy,* 151.
45. Lewis, *Horse and His Boy,* 151–152, 200.
46. Lewis, *Horse and His Boy,* 201. The passage is reminiscent of Thomas's encounter with Jesus in John 20:24-29. Of course, in Bree's case he does not doubt Aslan's resurrection as Thomas does of Jesus. Instead, Bree questions Aslan's true bestiality, making him more of a Gnostic (the Gnostics — believing that the flesh was corrupt and, hence, evil — did not believe that Jesus was truly incarnated but instead that He was only a

spirit). I have Will Vaus to thank for this insight on Bree.

47. Josh McDowell, *Evidence That Demands a Verdict* (San Bernardino, California: Here's Life, 1990), 11.
48. Lewis, *Horse and His Boy,* 201.This is not the first instance in which Lewis alludes to the idea of devouring in relation to God. Another significant mention of this theme is found in *The Silver Chair* when Jill Pole speaks with Aslan by a stream and asks him if he eats girls (22). Aslan's reply is seemingly metaphorical in nature, as he answers that he has indeed devoured individuals as well as places. Lewis may be underscoring the significance and all-encompassing experience of Christ in the life of a believer. Just as Aslan tells Jill that he has devoured individuals as well as whole kingdoms, so too Christ wants to devour our lives, but for our own good. It is a frightening and sobering thought for fallen human beings to comprehend, reminiscent of a passage often quoted by Lewis: "Whoever finds his life will lose it, and whoever loses his life for my [Christ's] sake will find it" (Matthew 10:39).
49. Lewis, *Mere Christianity,* 114.

CHAPTER 8

1. C. S. Lewis, *The Lion, the Witch and the Wardrobe* (New York: Harper Trophy, 2000), 12–22.
2. Sometimes repentance is associated with penance, but this is not a helpful connotation in terms of the writings of Lewis or the Bible.
3. C. S. Lewis, *Mere Christianity* (New York: Macmillan, 1952), 59.
4. C. S. Lewis, *The Abolition of Man* (New York: Macmillan, 1955).

5. Gordon R. Lewis and Bruce A. Demarest, *Integrative Theology* (Grand Rapids, MI: Zondervan, 1994), 3:87.
6. Leland Ryken, James C. Wilhoit, and Tremper Longman III, eds., *Dictionary of Biblical Imagery* (Downers Grove, IL: InterVarsity, 1998), under "Repentance."
7. Millard J. Erickson, *Christian Theology*, 2nd ed. (Grand Rapids, MI: Baker, 1998), 950.
8. C. S. Lewis, *The Magician's Nephew* (New York: Harper Trophy, 2000), 202.
9. C. S. Lewis, "Dangers of National Repentance," in *God in the Dock: Essays on Theology and Ethics,* ed. Walter Hooper (Grand Rapids, MI: Eerdmans, 1970), 189–192.
10. While biblical repentance need not be accompanied by weeping or other emotional expressions, such behavior is not precluded by the Bible. See, for example, Joel 2:12-13, where God calls His people to return to Him with "fasting and weeping and mourning."
11. For Tumnus's meeting with Lucy and his subsequent repentance, see chapter 2 of *The Lion, the Witch and the Wardrobe.*
12. C. S. Lewis, *Surprised by Joy: The Shape of My Early Life* (New York: Harcourt Brace, 1956), 237. Lewis's decision to follow Christ took place while he rode in the sidecar of his brother's motorcycle on the way to a zoo.
13. Lewis, *The Lion, the Witch and the Wardrobe*, 20.
14. Lewis, *The Lion, the Witch and the Wardrobe*, 46.
15. Lewis, *The Lion, the Witch and the Wardrobe*, 139, 178–180.
16. Lewis, *The Lion, the Witch and the Wardrobe*, 180–181.

17. Lewis, *The Lion, the Witch and the Wardrobe,* 184; C. S. Lewis, *The Voyage of the "Dawn Treader"* (New York: Harper Trophy, 2000), 111.
18. Eustace's experiences on Dragon Island are found in chapters 6 and 7 of *The Voyage of the "Dawn Treader."*
19. Lewis, *Voyage of the "Dawn Treader,"* 87, 91.
20. Lewis, *Voyage of the "Dawn Treader,"* 92, 101, 104.
21. Lewis, *Voyage of the "Dawn Treader,"* 110–111.
22. Lewis, *Voyage of the "Dawn Treader,"* 112.
23. Another term used to describe those who hold such a position is *exclusivist.*
24. Lewis was aware of the Hebrew meaning of Emeth. See C. S. Lewis, *Reflections on the Psalms* (New York: Harcourt, 1958), 60–61.
25. Recall the discussion in chapter 4, where it is mentioned that Shift attempts to blend the god Tash with Aslan as part of the ape's deception, resulting in Tashlan.
26. C. S. Lewis, *The Last Battle* (New York: Harper Trophy, 2000), 188–189.
27. Religious pluralists are sometimes referred to as universalists. For insights on religious pluralism from a particularist Christian perspective, see Harold Netland, *Encountering Religious Pluralism: The Challenge to Christian Faith and Mission* (Downers Grove, IL: InterVarsity, 2001); Harold Netland, *Dissonant Voices: Religious Pluralism and the Question of Truth* (Grand Rapids, MI: Eerdmans, 1991); and Ronald Nash, *Is Jesus the Only Savior?* (Grand Rapids, MI: Zondervan, 1994).
28. Lewis, *Last Battle,* 175–176.

29. The exchange between the two is reminiscent of the story of the woman at the well in John 4, where Jesus offered the woman "living water."
30. Lewis, *Silver Chair*, 23.
31. Stanley J. Grenz, David Guretzki, and Cherith Fee Nordling, *Pocket Dictionary of Theological Terms* (Downers Grove, IL: InterVarsity, 1999), under "inclusivism."
32. Lewis, *Mere Christianity*, 65.
33. Lewis, *Mere Christianity*, 176.
34. W. H. Lewis and Walter Hooper, eds., *Letters of C. S. Lewis*, rev. ed. (New York: Harcourt, 1993), 428, letter dated November 8, 1952. In this letter Lewis goes on to say that such speculations about unbelievers should lead Christians to pray for them and to live good lives as examples to others, so that non-Christians may be attracted to Christianity.
35. Winfried Corduan, *A Tapestry of Faiths: The Common Threads Between Christianity and World Religions* (Downers Grove, IL: InterVarsity, 2002), 161.
36. Aravis in *The Horse and His Boy* is another exception, but not in an inclusivist sense. Recall that Aravis flees Calormen of her own accord and chooses to live in Archenland — a kingdom near Narnia that honors Aslan.
37. Lewis, *Last Battle,* 188.
38. Lewis, *Magician's Nephew,* 174.
39. Lewis, *Horse and His Boy,* 214–215.
40. Lewis, *Horse and His Boy,* 216–217.
41. Lewis, *Last Battle,* 176. The fact that one of the renegade dwarfs who just a short time before the judgment of Aslan

was behaving most improperly by shooting and killing talking horses is allowed to enter Aslan's country emphasizes Lewis's belief that we cannot know who is saved or lost merely by outward appearances. Instead, God alone knows the heart.

42. Lewis, *Last Battle,* 83.
43. Lewis, *Last Battle,* 83. Other instances where the phrase appears are found on pages 137, 139, 144, and 169.
44. Lewis, *Last Battle,* 137.
45. Lewis, *Last Battle,* 166.
46. Lewis, *Last Battle,* 169. Aslan's words contrasting cunning with belief should not be taken to mean Lewis believed in unjustified belief or blind faith, as evident by Lewis's apologetic efforts (that is, the rational defense of Christianity).
47. C. S. Lewis, *The Great Divorce* (New York: Macmillan, 1946), 72. The dwarfs are not in "hell" in a Christian sense, but Lewis's point remains the same: If by choice one is closed to the truth, then the truth will be concealed.
48. Lewis, *Voyage of the "Dawn Treader,"* 112.
49. C. S. Lewis, "The Weight of Glory," in *The Weight of Glory and Other Addresses*, ed. Walter Hooper, rev. ed. (New York: Macmillan, 1980), 19.
50. Lewis, *Mere Christianity*, 66.
51. Jerry Bridges, *The Pursuit of Holiness* (Colorado Springs, CO: NavPress, 1978), 21–22.
52. This is evident, for instance, on page 142 of *Prince Caspian*, when Lucy alone sees Aslan and follows him but then puts down the others who did not believe her.

CONCLUSION

1. Augustine, *Confessions,* trans. R. S. Pine-Coffin (New York: Penguin, 1961), 21.
2. C. S. Lewis, *The Horse and His Boy* (New York: Harper Trophy, 2000), 163.
3. Lewis, 165.

APPENDIX

1. For a time Lewis owned a cat named Ginger. This is mentioned in C. S. Lewis, *Letters to an American Lady,* ed. Clyde S. Kilby (Grand Rapids, MI: Eerdmans, 2000), 72, letter dated February 22, 1958.

About *the* Author

Robert Velarde is an editor for Focus on the Family. An active member of several evangelical philosophy and theological organizations, he studied the works of C. S. Lewis at Denver Seminary. He is author of *Conversations with C. S. Lewis* and is pursuing graduate studies in philosophy via Southern Evangelical Seminary. Robert resides in Colorado Springs, Colorado, with his wife and four children.